A Midrash Reader

A Midrash Reader

Jacob Neusner

FORTRESS PRESS   MINNEAPOLIS

IN MEMORY OF

John A. Hollar

A MIDRASH READER

Internal design and typesetting: Polebridge Press

Cover design: Pollock Design Group

Library of Congress Cataloging-in-Publication Data

A Midrash reader / [compiled by] Jacob Neusner.
    p. cm.
    Includes bibliographical references.
    ISBN 0-8006-2433-5 (alk. paper)
    1. Midrash—Translations into English. I. Neusner, Jacob, 1932- .
BM512.M49 1990
296.1´40521–dc20   90-2995
                                                       CIP

Manufactured in the U.S.A.   1-2433

94   93   92   91   90   1   2   3   4   5   6   7   8   9   10

Contents

Acknowledgments

I consulted my colleagues, Ernest S. Frerichs and Wendell Dietrich, Brown University, and William Scott Green, University of Rochester, in the shaping of this book. I express my thanks to them for their observations and suggestions.

As this book was being edited, word came of the death of my editor at Fortress Press, Dr. John A. Hollar. He was a good editor for me, rich in ideas, patient with me as with everyone else, and devoted to my work. I offer this small tribute as a memorial of thanks for the presence that, for a time, he established in my life. For that I give thanks.

JACOB NEUSNER
Graduate Research Professor
of Religious Studies
University of South Florida
Tampa, Florida

Prologue

In *What Is Midrash?* I defined Midrash; here I place on display the principal documents that compile Midrash-exegesis and show how Midrash works in philosophy, theology, and morality. So while serving as a companion-anthology to *What Is Midrash?* this book stands on its own.

Although the faith conveyed by the Midrash-exegeses of Judaism requires intellect, this does not turn Scripture into a mere source of interesting facts or a set of propositions. Quite to the contrary, our capacity to reason and respond forms the resource of faith, as much as our capacity for faith itself. What does the use of intellect in search of God's message, in the Torah, for me, actually mean? The ancient rabbis read Scripture as God's personal letter to them. If you want to know what it means to read Scripture as if God had written it for you and to you personally, for your Israel and to all Israel here and now, then this book is for you. For I claim that in the sages of Judaism who produced the Midrash-compilations we find models for our own response to Scripture. They show us choices we may not have known we had. And once we see how they read Scripture, we can do no less. That is why, as I explain in chapter 1, what I display here is a point of far more than merely antiquarian interest in the study of classics of ancient Judaism. The Midrash-exegesis of the ancient sages of Judaism gives us a model for our own study of Scripture. And that is a separate task from the one of exposition and presentation that I undertook in *What Is Midrash?*

A second difference is that while there I introduced the subject Midrash in general, meaning scriptural exegesis and amplification, application and interpretation, this was in the setting of the diverse Judaisms of ancient times and how they interpreted Scripture or the Torah. But here I focus on Midrash as practiced by a particular Judaism in antiquity, the Judaism of the dual Torah.[1] That particular kind of

---

1. In my *Invitation to Midrash: A Teaching Book* (San Francisco: Harper & Row, 1988) I provide extensive abstracts, together with the Hebrew, for the character of the various Midrash-compilations. These several books complement one another, each serving its own purpose but also contributing toward a sustained introduction to, and representation of, the great Judaic tradition of scriptural study. The theory of the whole

Midrash-exegesis, contained in the Midrash-compilations accepted as canonical by the ancient rabbis, represents one species of the genus, interpretation of the Hebrew Scriptures. We do well to remember that there were other modes of scriptural exegesis and interpretation within the various Judaisms that in late antiquity inherited the Holy Scriptures of ancient Israel.[2] The particular context in which the sages of the Judaism of the dual Torah formed Midrash-compilations—what provoked them to do so, how an issue urgent in their own day compelled them to reconsider Scripture as Torah—is set forth in chapter 2.

The Midrash of other Judaisms deserves attention, of course, and that is why in *What Is Midrash?* I placed the variety of Midrash-exegesis produced by various Judaisms into a single context. These encompassed, for example, the Midrash-exegesis represented by the Greek-speaking exegetical tradition preserved in the Septuagint or by the Judaism portrayed in the writings of the Essene community of Qumran, or, for that matter, the Judaism represented by the Matthew's Gospel with its rich exegetical representation of the faith. The several exegetical approaches and traditions of the several Judaisms require attention, each in its own terms and context. After all, the word Midrash simply stands in Hebrew for the work of biblical exegesis and interpretation that is commonplace in all other languages.

But there are modes of scriptural exegesis that are quite particular to the Judaism of the dual Torah, just as there are media for reading and interpreting Scripture that are distinctive to Matthew's Gospel. In the shank of the book—parts 2 through 4—I show what these were through the representation of the text, context, and matrix of Midrash-compilations. These we see, therefore, in the larger intellectual setting of the system, the Judaism of the dual Torah, that produced these kinds of writings. To understand how the system has yielded the Midrash—in our terms, how the theology has generated the hermeneutic—we may call to mind the role and shape of Midrash in the Matthew's Gospel. We find only in Matthew's Judaic system the appeal to the life and teaching of Jesus called Christ as the interior reality to which all Scripture refers.

---

is presented in *Writing with Scripture: Biblical Exegesis and Theological Syllogism in Formative Judaism* [with William Scott Green] (Minneapolis: Fortress Press, 1989).

2. In speaking of Judaism(s), I do not refer to "the Bible," since the Bible consists of both the Old Testament and the New Testament. No Judaism—by definition—is biblical, since none includes as a holy book the New Testament writings. All Judaisms, as a matter of fact, appeal to the Torah, God's revelation to Israel, each one of them defining for itself the writings that fall into the classification of Torah. Hence throughout these pages, for the sake of clarity, I never refer to "the Bible" unless I mean the Bible in its entirety, as Christianity defined it.

And we find only in the Midrash-compilations of the Judaism of the dual Torah the appeal to the propositions that make that Judaism unique in its context as well. There is no technology of exegesis that is practiced by all Judaisms and no Christianities, and hence there is no "Jewish Midrash" that is different from "Christian Midrash" of the Hebrew Scriptures. What I draw for this anthology out of *What Is Midrash?* is only one thing, and even that is changed. It is the tripartite scheme of classification of Midrash-exegeses that I worked out there (as ideal types, of course) in terms of [1] paraphrase, [2] prophecy, and [3] parable. Within that structure I find a place for the Midrash-interpretations of all Judaisms of ancient times. Here, however, I drastically recast the meanings of the several categories and deal only with the Midrash-compilations of the dual Torah. The definition offered there serves here as well.

The word "Midrash" is generally used in three senses.

[1] It may refer to a compilation of scriptural exegeses, as in "the Midrash says," meaning, "the document contains the following. . . ."

[2] It may refer to an exegesis of Scripture, as in, "this Midrash shows us. . . ," meaning, "this interpretation of the verse at hand indicates. . . ."

[3] It may refer to a particular mode of scriptural interpretation, as in the phrase, "the Jewish Midrash holds. . . ," meaning (it is supposed) that a particular Judaic way of reading Scripture yields such-and-such result; or a particular hermeneutic identified with (a) Judaism teaches us to read in this way rather than in some other. In these pages I keep the three senses of the word separate from one another.

A brief definition of the Judaism of the dual Torah is in order at the outset; otherwise we do not grasp the intellectual and historical context in which Midrash-exegesis and Midrash-compilation took place within the Judaism of the dual Torah. The Judaism of the dual Torah is the one that appeals to the myth of divine revelation to Moses at Sinai of the Torah in two media, oral and written, hence "dual Torah." What distinguishes the Judaism at hand therefore is its doctrine of the dual media by which God's will for Israel, contained in the Torah revealed at Sinai, came down from ancient times.

Specifically, this Judaism maintains, when God revealed the Torah at Sinai, God transmitted the Torah in two media, one in writing, now contained in the Written Torah (which the Christian world calls "the Old Testament"). The other medium by which the Torah reached Israel was through memory, that is, the other Torah was transmitted orally and memorized by great prophets, then sages, down to the time of the sages of the age themselves. The writings that fall into the category of "the oral

Torah" then, together with the Hebrew Scripture ("Old Testament")
define the canon of that Judaism.
    This other, orally formulated and orally transmitted Torah—this
memorized Torah—characterizes this Judaism and no other. But the
oral Torah came to be written down, and, in the story of this Judaism, we
find the substance of the memorized Torah, that is to say, the oral Torah,
in the writings of the ancient rabbis of late antiquity. While referring to
an oral tradition that began at Sinai, these rabbis wrote their books from
ca. 200 to 600. The first document of this oral Torah was the Mishnah, a
philosophical law code closed at about the year 200 C[ommon] E[ra] [=
A.D.]. Further writings that fall into the classification of (oral) Torah
include the Tosefta, a collection of supplements to the Mishnah's laws, a
commentary to the Mishnah accomplished in the Land of Israel called
the Talmud of the Land of Israel, of about the year 400, a second such
commentary, done in the Jewish communities of Babylonia and called
the Talmud of Babylonia, of about the year 600, as well as commentaries
to the Written Torah by the sages of the age, such as Sifra, to Leviticus,
Sifré to Numbers, another Sifré, this one to Deuteronomy, of ca. 200–
300; then Genesis Rabbah, Leviticus Rabbah, and Pesiqta deRab
Kahana, of ca. 400–500; then Lamentations Rabbah, Ruth Rabbah,
Esther Rabbah, and Song of Songs Rabbah, of ca. 500–600.
    These three types of Midrash-compilations are all represented in the
pages of this anthology. I give sizable samples, laying stress, however, on
the Midrash-compilations that seem to me to demonstrate with great
power what it means to open Scripture and hear God's message for the
here and now of this morning. All of these other documents, encom-
passing both the Mishnah and its two great Talmuds, and the Midrash-
compilations contain the teachings of sages in late antiquity, from the
first through the sixth centuries of the Common Era. All together they
form that other, that oral Torah, that God revealed to Moses at Sinai.
These are the books that comprise the oral Torah, and here, for the
purposes explained presently, I provide an ample selection of what they
have to say as models for us of what it means to read Scripture as
something as fresh, compelling, and exciting as a personal letter that
came to us in this morning's mail.

1

Our Reasons

WHY STUDY MIDRASH AT ALL?

Religious people receive God's messages in many media. Christianity, Judaism, and Islam share the belief that one medium, and the critical one, is through writing, and hence we identify scripture—the Bible, the Quran, the Torah—as the principal, though not the sole, way that we learn what God wants us to know and do. And that means, in the nature of things, the scriptural religions appeal to intellect as the vehicle for response to, and service of, God. And that brings us not solely to Scripture, the Hebrew part of the Christian Bible, the written part of the dual Torah (oral and written) of Christianity and Judaism respectively. For how we use our minds to form an intellectual response to not God in the abstract, but God's word in the concrete form of scripture—the Bible, the Torah—guides us to the knowledge of God. And Midrash is the way that the sages of the Judaism of the dual Torah set forth what they knew, which is, how to read Scripture to gain access to Torah, God's revelation in the dual Torah.

Why are their modes of thought and inquiry important to us? Because we today, Jews and Christians, receive the Hebrew Scriptures as God's word to us, we ask how others sharing that same conviction have made and now make that word their own. For the task of all scriptural study is to make sense of eternity for the here and now, the moment at which we (in the language of Judaism) receive the Torah ourselves. In Midrash we see how sages, living in challenging times, reread Scripture so as to learn what God wanted of them that day, that hour. This acutely contemporary response to Scripture provides us with models for our own approach to the Hebrew Scriptures.

Not historical scholarship but faithful response of believers who also were scholars and intellectuals—and that is precisely what the sages of Judaism were—shows us a model of the way to receive as the word for this day, and to respond in heart and mind and faith to Scripture. And whether we read the ancient Israelite writings as the Old Testament in the setting of Christian faith, or as the written Torah in light of the oral Torah, in the setting of Judaic faith, the task remains the same. So our interest in the sages of Judaism in these pages derives from our interest in Scripture. Readers of these pages, so I assume, take up the ancient Israelite holy books because they believe, as I believe, and as the sages of the Torah, the rabbis of Judaism, believed and now affirm, that here we find God's word and will for us. Then all of us, then and now, in Christianity and Judaism, must ask for models for ourselves in forming our response to Scripture.

In the rabbis who produced the Midrash-compilations laid out in these pages we find an example of how, faced with challenge from without and crisis from within,[1] great sages found in Scripture the wisdom and the truth that guided them. Rabbis, priests, ministers, believing Jews and Christians come to Scripture today with the burdens of the hour.

I offer the sages of Judaism as a paradigm not because I think any of us can rehearse their specific modes of thought or recapitulate their particular conclusions. For Christians that is manifestly not possible. And for Jews too the model and the medium prove compelling, but the message requires modification in light of the age that we confront. Rather, so I maintain, the Judaic sages show us media of making choices that we can make our own, modes of thought that, properly modified to accommodate the intellectual requirements of our own circumstance, prove remarkably pertinent. If we want to know how people read Scripture who believe that through it God speaks to the most acutely contemporary issues, the enduring tensions of the everyday, here is the chance to find out.

What we shall find out about them is defined entirely in the measures of their own time and circumstance. We cannot pretend that we lived then, or that they live forever. But when we understand their questions and how they brought forth their answers, we gain access to a model for ourselves: a paradigm, if not a detailed pattern, for how people can use, and have used, their intellects in responding to the imperatives of Scripture in framing an answer to the urgent questions of their age. The Midrash-compilations of the Judaism of the dual Torah, laid out in the

1. In chapter 2 I spell out both the intellectual crisis that precipitated the composition of the earlier Midrash-compilations, Sifra, the two Sifrés, for example, and the political crisis that provoked the compilation of the later Midrash-compilations, Leviticus Rabbah, Genesis Rabbah, and onward.

pages that follow, show us thoughtful people answering urgent questions through the encounter with Scripture, turning Scripture into Torah, revelation. When we see what and how they did so, we can see in a new light our own quest for God in Scripture: from words to the revealed Word, that is, the word revealed in particular to us.

That explains why I place on display how the sages of Judaism undertook three of the most important tasks that any faithful Jew or Christian must accomplish in response to Scripture. It is first, to hear the message of Scripture, that is, to master the text; second, to interpret the message of Scripture, that is, to find the correct context; and finally, to make our own the meaning of Scripture, that is, to identify the proper matrix in which to receive (in the language of Judaism) the Torah, or (in the language of Christianity) God's word. (And the two languages are virtually identical in sense and substance.) So we move from text, to context, to matrix, led by the sages who provide a paradigm for the dynamic reading of Scripture. Let me explain what that means.

First, we have to make sure we understand what the document says, and that is the matter of text, though I use the word "text" not in the narrow sense of the wording of the document, but its fundamental message: What precisely is it saying? And this is not accomplished through mere philology, knowledge of Hebrew, the archaeology of the Land of Israel, and other interesting subjects. To know what the Scripture says, we have to read Scripture as the text of our faith. And that means, for Judaism then and now, to read Scripture as Torah, God's revelation to Israel, the holy people. For just what amplifying and clarifying and paraphrasing Scripture must require finds definition only within the framework of the life and faith of people for whom the document requires that amplification. And that is defined by the text of faith, which then imposes upon Scripture the standing and importance that it enjoys. In the case of Judaism, it is to investigate what I call the textuality of the Torah.

Second, from the inner realm of the faith that identifies Scripture as Torah (for Judaism) or the Old Testament as part of the Bible (for Christianity) we move to the world beyond, the context in which the text locates itself. When people open the Scriptures, oftentimes it is to know what should be, what should happen, what things mean. The context of Scripture then is not the past but the present, and more compellingly still, the future. That interest in the future as revealed in Scripture takes diverse forms. Here the ancient sages of Judaism provide a powerful example of how, with all due respect for the pastness of the past, people could make sense of the world they knew, and therefore also discern the outlines of the world coming upon them, in the pages of Scripture. It is the reading of Scripture as prophecy that defines the context in which Scripture is received as the work of the Holy Spirit, in Judaism, God's word, in Christianity. So our sages provide a paradigm for how we may achieve the clarification of Scripture in the light of the future.

Third, from a clear account of the future that we envision, we gain perspective on the present that we endure—but also shape. And the Judaic sages show us one way in which to see the everyday as a recapitulation of Scripture in the here and the now. Seeing an event in the street, they perceived a rehearsal of an event in Scripture. Or they understood the event and its meaning in the model of what they deemed to be Scripture's counterpart and parable. So they formed a single eternity out of disparate time, their present and the past of history. Through scriptural study they accomplished that recasting of the here and the now into the model of eternity. So they approached Scripture not only to help them see the everyday as recapitulation of Scripture but also, and I think of equal consequence, to see Scripture as the matrix for the everyday. They took the position that we understand Scripture better than did a generation before us, as they understood matters better than did their predecessors, for each succeeding age knows more than the one before about God's plan for all time and all humanity. We are not wiser because we know more, but in the pages of Scripture we may become wiser by understanding better what we know.

In the Midrash-interpretations of Scripture that are set forth here, we see a way of reading Scripture that for most people is otherwise unknown. But properly understood, the Judaic sages, not different from ourselves, are bringing to Scripture questions of text, context, and matrix, issues of the everyday read in light of the Torah, a quest for future history, a concern for the right reading of the here and now. They then show us a model we did not know we had. When we work through the writings of the Judaic sages, we gain access to choices we did not possess before we took the trouble to follow, in their own program of interpretation and in line with their own propositions as well, people doing in their way things that we wish to do in ours.

2

Their Reasons

WHEN, WHERE, AND WHY DID THE JUDAIC
SAGES MAKE MIDRASH?

Compiling books of scriptural-exegesis—that is, Midrash-compila-tions—forms a chapter in the formative history of the Judaism of the dual Torah. Other Judaisms, of course, made Midrash-exegeses and compiled them in books, and through these compilations they made important points. The Judaism of the dual Torah began with another kind of writing than the composition of Midrash-exegeses of Scripture and the compiling of those exegeses into commentaries on scriptural books. Only after the work of exegesis of a document distinct from Scripture did the sages of that Judaism turn, also, to Scripture and ask pressing questions about it. In order to follow the history of the making of books of just that kind, we must tell the story of the impact of the appearance of a holy book beyond Scripture upon the lives and thought of the people who deemed that book to be as holy and as authoritative as Scripture.

I refer to the Mishnah, a philosophical law code that reached closure at about 200 C.E. [=A.D.] and soon afterward was represented as part of the Torah God had revealed to Moses at Sinai. This component of the Torah represented revelation that was orally formulated and orally trans-mitted for a long time, so it was maintained, and only now formalized in the Mishnah, which itself was orally formulated and orally transmitted. The advent of the Mishnah in circa 200 demanded that people explain the status and authority of the new document. The Mishnah rapidly was accorded the status of the authoritative law-code of Judaism; it enjoyed the sponsorship of the Jewish autonomous governor, the ruler of the ethnic group ("ethnarch" or "patriarch") of the Jews of Palestine, who knew themselves, of course, as Israel in the Land of Israel. And from that time onward, for those subject to the authority of the Roman-recognized

Jewish government, the Mishnah, alongside Scripture, was not only authoritative, it was authoritative just as was Scripture: it was Torah.

Because, at its very beginnings the Mishnah was turned into an authoritative law code, the constitution (along with Scripture) of Israel in its Land, it forthwith made its move into the politics, courts, and bureaus of the Jewish government of the Land of Israel. Men (never women, until our own day) who mastered the Mishnah thereby qualified themselves as judges and administrators in the government of Judah the Patriarch as well as in the government of the Jewish community of Babylonia. Over the next three hundred years, the Mishnah served as the foundation for the Talmuds' formation of the system of law and theology we now know as Judaism. Exegesis of the Mishnah furthermore defined the taxonomy for hermeneutics of Scripture.

The Mishnah therefore demanded explanation, both on its own terms and also in relationship to the Torah, that is, Scripture. What is this book? How does it relate to the (written) Torah revealed to Moses at Mount Sinai? Under whose auspices, and by what authority, does the law of the Mishnah govern the life of Israel? These questions bear political as well as theological implications. But, to begin with, the answers to theological questions emerge out of an enterprise of exegesis, of literature. The reception of the Mishnah followed several distinct lines, each of them symbolized by a particular sort of book. One line of response addressed the Mishnah on its own terms. It led from the exegesis of the Mishnah to the amplification and compilation of these exegeses in the two Talmuds. The other line of response began with the question of the relationship of the Mishnah to Scripture. That question soon broadened into a full-scale rereading of important books of Scripture. The result was the development of Midrash-exegeses which were brought together in Midrash-compilations. For the next four centuries the study of the Mishnah and of Scripture would occupy the attention of the best minds of Israel, the authorities of the two Talmuds and of the numerous Midrash-compilations.

One line from the Mishnah therefore stretched through the Tosefta—a supplement to the Mishnah—and the two Talmuds, one formed in the Land of Israel, the other in Babylonia, both serving as exegesis and amplification of the Mishnah. Thus the stages were [1] Mishnah, ca. 200, then [2] the Tosefta, ca. 300, [3] the Talmud of the Land of Israel, ca. 400, and [4] the Talmud of Babylonia, ca. 600.

The second line flowed from the Mishnah to compilations of biblical exegesis of three different stages, marked by three distinct sorts of compilations. The work began with the reading of Scripture in relationship to the Mishnah and the Tosefta, but then broadened to the reading of Scripture as a focus in its own terms.

First, there were exegetical collections framed partly in relation to the Mishnah and the Tosefta, in particular Sifra on Leviticus, Sifré on Numbers, and Sifré on Deuteronomy. These compilations fall into the second and third centuries, down to ca. 300. These compilations served to answer the initial questions precipitated by the advent of the Mishnah: How is the Mishnah (part of the) Torah?

But matters did not end here. Once people made Midrash-compilations, they turned to other books of Scripture, or went over the same books they had already dealt with, now with a new range of questions in mind. Just as the two Talmuds not only amplified the Mishnah but also generalized and introduced fresh ranges of inquiry, so the Midrash-compilations of the second and third stages moved outward from the Mishnah to a new level of speculation about Scripture. The second phase encompassed exegetical collections organized mainly in relation to Scripture, with special reference to Genesis and Leviticus, in Genesis Rabbah and Leviticus Rabbah. These are to be dated ca. 400–450. These compilations responded not to the intellectual crisis of the Mishnah but to the political crisis of the events of the fourth century, marked as they were by the triumph of Christianity and the permanent subordination of Judaism as relic. The political success of Christianity made acute the question of God's plan for Israel. These documents reread Genesis to produce a theory of history and its laws, and Leviticus to yield a theory of society and its rules.

Leviticus Rabbah, in particular, moved from verse-by-verse exegesis to abstract, propositional argument through the medium of Scripture. And alongside that document came exegetical collections focused on constructing abstract discourse out of diverse verses of Scripture but on a single theme or problem, represented by Pesikta de Rab Kahana (ca. 450–500). In that compilation the liturgy defines the proposition, and topical expositions of important theological propositions are set forth, with ample citation of Scripture. And that document forms the bridge to the final category of Midrash-compilations.

This third sort were thematic collections, made in response to synagogue liturgy, which on specified occasions read given books of the Scripture. But the liturgy was thematic—suffering and disaster for the ninth of Ab, on which the book of Lamentations is read; renewal and rebirth for the advent of Passover, on which the Song of Songs is read; salvation in a time of disaster for the holiday of Purim, on which the book of Esther is read; conversion to the Torah and the coming of the

Messiah for Pentecost, which celebrates the giving of the Torah, on which the book of Ruth is read. Thus the liturgy focused upon the exposition of great problems or topics, and, through the amplification of a given scriptural book, these themes were realized through Scripture.

This simple catalog of the types, range, and volume of creative writing over the three hundred years from the closure of the Mishnah indicates an obvious fact. The Mishnah stands at the beginning of a new and stunningly original epoch in the formation of Judaism. Like such generative crises as the return to Zion for the nation as a whole and the advent of Jesus for his family and followers, the advent of the Mishnah, in the aftermath of the destruction of the Temple of Jerusalem in 70 and the defeat of the war fought to regain the city and rebuild the Temple in 132–134, ignited in Israel a great burst of energy. The extraordinary power of the Mishnah, moreover, is seen in its very lonely position in Israelite holy literature of its time and afterward. The subsequent literature, for centuries to come, would refer back to the Mishnah or stand in some clear-cut hermeneutical relationship to it. But for its part, the Mishnah referred to nothing prior to itself—except (and then, mostly implicitly and by indirection) to Scripture. So from the Mishnah back to the revelation of God to Moses at Sinai—in the view of the Mishnah— lies a vast desert. But from the Mishnah forward stretches a fertile plain.

The crisis precipitated by the Mishnah therefore stimulated wide-ranging speculation, experiments of a theological character, yielding vast initiatives of hermeneutics expressed in literary and (in the nature of things) therefore also of a political thought and expression. The work of defining and explaining the Mishnah in relation to the (written) Torah, interpreting the meaning of the Mishnah, expanding upon and applying its laws, was accompanied by the making, also, of compilations of exegeses of Scripture. The formation of the Talmuds and scriptural-exegetical collections thus made necessary—indeed, urgent—extraordinary and original reflection on the definition of the Torah, through inquiry into the nature of canon and scriptural authority, the range and possibilities of revelation. The results of that work all together would then define Judaism from that time to this. So the crisis presented opportunity. And Israel's sages took full advantage of the occasion. That is why I offer them as an example of how people have received Scripture as a personal letter from God to them—written and delivered this morning!

What, then, was this crisis? Let me begin the tale by returning to the Mishnah itself. I must first of all explain why and how the Mishnah presented such an unprecedented problem to the patriarch's sages who received the Mishnah. It is easy to do so in a way accessible to people to whom all of these events and writings have been, up to now, entirely unknown or, if known, alien and incomprehensible. To phrase the theological question so that anyone in the West may grasp it, I need simply point out one fact. So far as Judaism was concerned, revelation had been contained in the Hebrew Scriptures later on called the written Torah. True, God may have spoken in diverse ways. The last of the biblical books had been completed—so far as Jews then knew—many centuries before. How, then, could a new book now claim standing as holy and revealed by God? What validated the authority of the people who knew and applied that holy book to Israel's life? These questions would define the critical issue of formative Judaism, from 200 to 600. The resolution of the problem defines Judaism today.

Accordingly, the crisis precipitated by the Mishnah came about because of the urgent requirement of explaining, first, just what the Mishnah was in relation to the Torah of Moses; second, why the sages who claimed to interpret and apply the law of the Mishnah to the life of Israel had the authority to do so; and, third, how Israel, in adhering to the rules of the Mishnah, kept the will of God and lived the holy life God wanted them to live. And that brings us to the first of the three stages in the formation of the Midrash-compilations: the age of paraphrase.

PART ONE

Paraphrase and the Text of Scripture

THE AMPLIFICATION OF SCRIPTURE
IN THE CONTEXT OF THE TORAH

3

Prologue

THE AMPLIFICATION OF SCRIPTURE
IN THE CONTEXT OF THE TORAH

It is the crisis precipitated by the Mishnah's advent as an authoritative and holy book that ultimately led to the formation of Midrash-compilations in the Judaism of the dual Torah. And the first stage in these compilations is characterized by the address to three questions:

1. a sustained amplification of the sense of Scripture
2. an account of the relationship of the Mishnah to Scripture
3. a picture of the information provided by Scripture, now reassembled in a systematic and well-organized way.

All of these tasks involved the encounter with the sense of Scripture, read pretty much in its own terms. Only later on were issues brought to Scripture that required the reading of Scripture through not amplifying and extending its meaning, but rather treating its sense as somehow prophetic, and still later as parabolic. The prophetic Scripture would speak of an age later than that which the narrative seemed to suggest: specifically, our day. The Scripture turned into existential parable would recast Scripture's teachings and narrative into an account of everywhere and all time. But these revisionings of Scripture lay far in the future. The first task, the task of reading and amplifying the text, was addressed by the authorships and compilers of works on four scriptural books: Leviticus, Numbers, Deuteronomy, and Exodus (in the order in which we shall meet the Midrash-compilations). And the entire work began, as I have said, with the critical task of receiving and finding a context for this new document, the Mishnah.

Now why should the Mishnah in particular have presented these critical problems of a social and theological order? After all, from the closure of Scripture to the end of the second century it was hardly the first piece of new writing to confront Israel with the claim of authority and therefore holiness: God's word. Other books speaking to other Judaisms had found a capacious place in the canon of the groups of Israelites that received them and deemed them holy. The canon of Judaisms that had taken shape over the centuries, though not the Judaism of the dual Torah, had made room for writings we call the apocryphal and pseudepigraphic books, for instance. The Essene library at Qumran encompassed a diverse group of writings, surely received as authoritative and holy, that other Jews did not know within their canon. So, as is clear, we have to stand back and ask why, of the sages who received and realized the Mishnah, that book should have presented special, particularly stimulating, problems.

Framing matters as I do, I ask in particular, Why should the issue of the *relation* of the Mishnah to Scripture have proved so pressing in the circles of talmudic rabbis of the third, fourth, and fifth centuries? After all, we have no evidence that the relation to the canon of Scripture of the Manual of Discipline, the Hymns, the War Scroll, or the Damascus Covenant perplexed the teacher of righteousness and the other holy priests of the Essene community. To the contrary, those documents at Qumran appear side by side with the ones we now know as canonical Scripture. The high probability is that, to the Essenes, the sectarian books were no less holy and authoritative than Leviticus, Deuteronomy, Nahum, Habakkuk, Isaiah, and the other books of the biblical canon that they, among all Israelites, revered.

The issue had to be raised because of the peculiar traits of the Mishnah itself. But the dilemma proved acute, not merely chronic, because of the particular purpose the Mishnah was meant to serve and because of the political sponsorship behind the document. As I said above, the Mishnah was to provide Israel's constitution. It was promulgated by the patriarch—the ethnic ruler—of the Jewish nation in the Land of Israel, Judah the Patriarch, who ruled with Roman support as the fully recognized Jewish authority in the Holy Land. So the Mishnah was public, not sectarian, nor merely idle speculation of a handful of Galilean rabbinical philosophers, though in structure and content that is precisely what it was.

The Mishnah emerged as a political document. It demanded assent and conformity to its rules, where they were relevant to the government and court system of the Jewish people in its land. So the Mishnah could not be ignored and therefore had to be explained in universally accessible terms. Furthermore, the Mishnah demanded explanation not merely in relation to the established canon of Scripture and apology as the constitution of the Jew's government, the patriarchate of second-century Land of Israel. The nature of Israelite life, lacking all capacity to distinguish as secular any detail of the common culture, made it natural to wonder about a deeper issue. Israel understood its collective life and the fate of each individual under the aspect of God's loving concern, as expressed in the Torah.

Accordingly, laws issued to define what people were supposed to do could not stand by themselves; they had to receive the imprimatur of Heaven, that is, they had to be given the status of revelation. Accordingly, to make its way in Israelite life, the Mishnah as a constitution and code demanded for itself a theory of beginnings at (or in relation to) Sinai, with Moses, from God. As was pointed out above, other new writings for a long time had proved able to win credence as part of the Torah, hence as revealed by God and so enjoying legitimacy. But they did so in ways not taken by the Mishnah's framers. How did the Mishnah differ?

It was in the medium of writing that, in the view of all of Israel until about 200, God had been understood to reveal the divine word and will. The Torah was a written book. People who claimed to receive further messages from God usually wrote them down. They had three choices in securing acceptance of their account. All three involved linking the new to the old. In claiming to hand on revelation, they could, first, sign their books with the names of biblical heroes. Second, they could imitate the style of biblical Hebrew. Third, they could present an exegesis of existing written verses, validating their ideas by supplying proof texts for them. From the closure of the Torah literature in the time of Ezra, circa 450 B.C. to the time of the Mishnah, nearly seven hundred years later, we do not have a single book alleged to be holy and at the same time standing wholly out of relationship to the Holy Scriptures of ancient Israel. The pseudepigraphic writings fall into the first category, the Essene writings at Qumran into the second and third. We may point also to the Gospels, which take as a principal problem demonstrating how Jesus had fulfilled the prophetic promises of the Old Testament and in other ways carried forward and even embodied Israel's Scripture.

Insofar as a piece of Jewish writing did not find a place in relationship to Scripture, its author laid no claim to present a holy book. The contrast between Jubilees and the Testaments of the Patriarchs, with their constant and close harping on biblical matters, and the several books of Maccabees, shows the differences. The former claim to present God's revealed truth; the latter, history. So a book was holy because in style, in

authorship, or in (alleged) origin it continued Scripture, finding a place
therefore (at least in the author's mind) within the canon, or because it
provided an exposition on Scripture's meaning.

But the Mishnah made no such claim. It entirely ignored the style of
biblical Hebrew, speaking in a quite different kind of Hebrew altogether.
It is silent on its authorship through sixty-two of the sixty-three tractates
(the claims of Abot pose a special problem). In any event, nowhere does
the Mishnah contain the claim that God had inspired the authors of the
document. These are not given biblical names and certainly are not
alleged to have been biblical saints. Most of the book's named authorities
flourished within the same century as its anonymous arrangers and
redactors, not in remote antiquity. Above all, the Mishnah contains
scarcely a handful of exegeses of Scripture. These, where they occur,
play a trivial and tangential role. So here is the problem of the Mishnah:
different from Scripture in language and style, indifferent to the claim of
authorship by a biblical hero or divine inspiration, stunningly aloof from
allusion to verses of Scripture for nearly the whole of its discourse—yet
authoritative for Israel.

So the Mishnah was not a statement of theory alone, telling only how
things will be in the eschaton. Nor was it a wholly sectarian document,
reporting the view of a group without standing or influence in the larger
life of Israel. True, in some measure it bears both of these traits of
eschatology and sectarian provenance. But the Mishnah was (and is) law
for Israel. It entered the government and courts of the Jewish people,
both in the motherland and also overseas, as the authoritative constitution of the courts of Judaism. The advent of the Mishnah therefore
marked a turning in the life of the nation-religion. The document
demanded explanation and apology!

The one thing one could not do, as a Jew in third-century Tiberias,
Sepphoris, Caesarea, or Beth Shearim, in Galilee, was ignore the thing.
True, one might refer solely to ancient Scripture and tradition, and live
life out within the inherited patterns of the familiar Israelite religion-
culture. But as soon as one dealt with the Jewish government in charge
of everyday life—went to court over the damages done to a crop by a
neighbor's ox, for instance—one came up against a law in addition to the
law of Scripture, a document the principles of which governed and
settled all matters. So the Mishnah rapidly came to confront the life of
Israel. The people who knew the Mishnah, the rabbis or sages, came to
dominate that life. And their claim, in accord with the Mishnah, to
exercise authority and the right to impose heavenly sanction came to
perplex. Now the crisis is fully exposed.

The Mishnah therefore made necessary the formation of the Talmuds, its exegetical companions. Within the processes of exegesis of the Mishnah came the labor of collecting and arranging these exegeses, in correlation with the Mishnah, read line by line and paragraph by paragraph. The sorts of things the sages who framed the Talmuds did to the Mishnah, they then went and did to Scripture. Within the work of exegesis of Scripture was the correlative labor of organizing what had been said verse by verse, following the structure of a book of the Hebrew Bible. The type of discourse and the mode of organizing the literary result of discourse suitable for the one document served the other as well. The same people did both for the same reasons. So to the Tosefta, Sifra, and the Yerushalmi alike, the paramount issue was Scripture, not merely its authority but especially its sheer mass of information. The decisive importance of the advent of the Mishnah in precipitating the vast exegetical enterprise represented by the books at hand emerges from a simple fact. The documents all focus attention on the Mishnah in particular. Two of them, the Tosefta and the Yerushalmi, organize everything at hand around the redactional structure supplied by the Mishnah itself.

Let me skip ahead to the end of the story, since in these pages we shall have no reason to attend to the final shape of canonical writings, supplied by the Talmud of Babylonia or Bavli at ca. 600, after the Midrash-compilations we consider had come to closure. The importance of the Bavli's distinctive contribution now becomes entirely clear. The Bavli carried forward a long-established enterprise, namely, the forging of links between the Mishnah and Scripture. But the organizers and redactors of the materials compiled in the Bavli did something unprecedented. They allowed sustained passages of Scripture to serve, as much as sustained and not merely episodic passages of the Mishnah served, as main beams in the composition of structure and order. In a single document, the Mishnah and Scripture functioned together and for the first time in much the same way. The original thesis, that the Mishnah depended upon the written Torah, thus all of its statements were linked to proof texts of Scripture, now gave way to its natural and complete fulfillment. Once sets of verses of Scripture could be isolated and made, in all of their continuity, to provide a focus of discourse just as the Mishnah did, Scripture would join the Mishnah in a single statement, cut down and reshaped to conform to the model of the Mishnah.

So Scripture now joined the Mishnah in a new union, in mythic language, one whole Torah. In so revising Scripture as to recast it into that same discursive and rhetorical framework that defined how and where the Mishnah would serve, the authors—framers of larger-scale units of discourse, ultimate redactors alike—made their unique contribution. Imposing a literary and redactional unity upon documents so remarkably disparate in every respect as the Mishnah and Scripture, the Bavli's authors created something both entirely their own and in no way original to them: Judaism in its final and complete statement, Judaism in conclusion. From this point forward, the Torah would expand and develop, but only by making its own and naturalizing within its realm initially alien modes of thought and bodies of truth. Of these, two must be taken into account: philosophy in the Greco-Islamic tradition, and mysticism. We now turn to ask how the Torah made its own these two important sources of religious truth. And that question draws us back to our task: the presentation of Midrash-compilations in their sequence and types.

4

Sifré to Numbers
and Sifré to Deuteronomy

APPLYING THE TORAH
TO THE EVERYDAY WORLD

The first encounter with Scripture demands that we make sense of its straightforward statements. For before we can hope to discover a message for our circumstance, we have to find the message that is there at the start. And this work of elucidation may yield compelling messages, even without our inserting ourselves into the process of amplification and application. A principal interest of the earlier compilations of Midrash-exegeses, in Sifré to Numbers and Sifré to Deuteronomy, is to join in the discourse of Scripture, meaning, to make oneself part of the conversation. This is done by bringing to bear the sorts of questions that a listener will direct to the speaker in a dialogue: "Do you mean that in general, or only concerning the specific case? What is the sense of that phrase? In other words, do you maintain . . ." and similar matters. Application to the everyday world commences when translation into the framework of the here and the now is undertaken. Our task to begin with is to see the repertoire of methods that guide the exegete-theologian: What are the choices, and how does one choose? For that purpose, we review a variety of readings provided by Sifré to Numbers. Then we shall examine a sustained and unbroken reading of a complete passage, as the authors of Sifré to Deuteronomy walk us through an important scriptural law.

Here is a sample of how, in Sifré to Numbers, a sustained reading of the book of Numbers, that work is done. The first passage, which I number I:I.1, meaning, the opening unit of the document, the opening chapter of the unit, the opening completed proposition of the chapter; then A, B, and onward mark the smallest whole units of thought (e.g., sentences); these are passages that cannot be further subdivided without losing any meaning at all. So we move from the whole to the parts, and, in other approaches than the one set forth here, identifying each component of a passage allows us to undertake certain analytical work that we cannot do if we do not know what we conceive to be the bits and pieces of a composition.

At I:I:1 we ask why a passage is set forth at all: What sense does the Torah wish here to convey? At issue is the repetition of the same matter in two separate places, and the solution is to find a distinct purpose for each point at which the rule is expressed. The exegetical focus, then, is on the larger composite of Scripture, rather than on a word-for-word explication of what is at hand. The exegete-compositors want to know how one passage serves a distinct purpose. The pericope is continuous and unitary.

Sifré to Numbers Chapter One, to Numbers 5:1–4

I:I

1. A. "The Lord said to Moses, 'Command the people of Israel that they put out of the camp [every leper and every one having a discharge, and every one that is unclean through contact with the dead]'" (Num. 5:1–2).
   B. For what purpose is this passage presented?
   C. Because it is said, "But the man who is unclean and does not cleanse himself [that person shall be cut off from the midst of the assembly, since he has defiled the sanctuary of the Lord, because the water for impurity has not been thrown upon him, he is unclean]" (Num. 19:20).
   D. Consequently, we are informed of the penalty [for contaminating the sanctuary]. But where are we informed of the admonition not to do so?
   E. Scripture accordingly states, "Command the people of Israel that they put out of the camp every leper and every one having a discharge, and every one that is unclean through contact with the dead" (Num. 5:1–2).
   F. Lo, here is an admonition that unclean persons not come into the sanctuary ["out of the camp"] in a state of uncleanness. [Consequently, the entire transaction—admonition, then penalty—is laid forth.]

In the second passage of the same major unit, we interpret the language in a philological essay of which any member of the American Oriental Society would be legitimately proud. The point of interest now is in the sense of the word "command." The demonstration will focus upon evidence of a variety of verses of Scripture that "command" refers both for the present instant and for generations to come. No one, then, can maintain that the commandments apply only in the distant past. The exegesis of the verse at hand hardly forms the focus of interest at all. The same point can have been introduced in the exegesis of any of the proof texts that are laid before us. Not only so, but the base verse before us does not even come first in the repertoire of proof texts. So the composition has been worked out in its own terms and only afterward selected for this, among other, positions. The same is so for Ishmael's proof. The upshot is that the purpose of the pericope is to make a point applicable in general, and the passage falls into the classification of a syllogism, not an exegesis of a particular verse. And that shows us how the framers of Midrash-exegesis moved beyond the limits of the particular verse under discussion. One of their important projects was to seek general propositions, which would guide them in reading a variety of passages—which is to say, to come up with explanations for discrete facts.

I:II

1. A. "Command" (Num. 5:2):
    B. The commandment at hand is meant both to be put into effect immediately and also to apply for generations to come.
    C. You maintain that the commandment at hand is meant both to be put into effect immediately and also to apply for generations to come.
    D. But perhaps the commandment is meant to apply only after a time [but not right away, at the moment at which it was given].
    E. [We shall now prove that the formulation encompasses both generations to come and also the generation to whom the commandment is entrusted.] Scripture states, "The Lord said to Moses, 'Command the people of Israel that they put out [of the camp every leper and every one having a discharge, and every one that is unclean through contact with the dead. You shall put out both male and female, putting them outside the camp, that they may not defile their camp, in the midst of which I dwell.'] And the people of Israel did so and drove them outside the camp, as the Lord said to Moses, *so the people of Israel did*" (Gen. 5:1–4). [The verse itself makes explicit the fact that the requirement applied forthwith, not only later on.]
    F. Lo, we have learned that the commandment at hand is meant to be put into effect immediately.
    G. How then do we derive from Scripture the fact that it applies also for generations to come? [We shall now show that the same word used here, *command*, pertains to generations to come and not only to the generation at hand.]
    H. Scripture states, "Command the children of Israel to bring you pure oil from beaten olives [for the lamp, that a light may be kept burning

continually outside the veil of the testimony in the tent of meeting,
Aaron shall keep it in order from evening to morning before the Lord
continually; it shall be a statute for ever throughout your genera-
tions]" (Lev. 24:2).

I. Lo, we here derive evidence that the commandment at hand is meant
    both to be put into effect immediately and also to apply for genera-
    tions to come [based on the framing of the present commandment].

J. How, then, do we derive evidence that all of the commandments that
    are contained in the Torah [apply in the same way]? [We wish now to
    prove that the language, *command*, always bears the meaning imputed
    to it here.]

K. R. Ishmael maintained, "Since the bulk of the commandments stated
    in the Torah are presented without further amplification, while in the
    case of one of them [namely, the one at hand], Scripture has given
    explicit details, that commandment [that has been singled out] is
    meant both to be put into effect immediately and also to apply for
    generations to come. Accordingly, I apply to all of the other com-
    mandments in the Torah the same detail, so that in all cases the
    commandment is meant both to be put into effect immediately and
    also to apply for generations to come."

The third passage is of the same sort as the second. Once more we
wish to generalize from one passage to a variety of passages, and from
several passages we wish to produce a coherent rule or proposition. The
three points at hand hardly pertain to our verse in particular. They form
general comments on the meaning of the word "command," just as in
the former case. The reason for the inclusion of this syllogistic discourse
is at D, which clearly intersects with our passage.

I.III

1. A. R. Judah b. Beterah says, "The effect of a commandment stated in any
        context serves only [1] to lend encouragement.

    B. "For it is said, 'But command Joshua and encourage and strengthen
        him' (Deut. 3:28).

    C. "Accordingly, we derive the lesson that strength is granted only to the
        strong, and encouragement only to the stout of heart."

    D. R. Simeon b. Yohai says, "The purpose of a commandment in any
        context is only [2] to deal with the expenditure of money, as it is said,
        'Command the children of Israel to bring you pure oil from beaten
        olives for the lamp, that a light may be kept burning continually
        outside the veil of the testimony in the tent of meeting, Aaron shall
        keep it in order from evening to morning before the Lord continually;
        it shall be a statute for ever throughout your generations' (Lev. 24:2).
        'Command the people of Israel that they put out of the camp every

leper and every one having a discharge, and every one that is unclean through contact with the dead' (Num. 5:1-2). 'Command the children of Israel that they give to the Levites from the inheritance of their possession cities to dwell in, and you shall give to the Levites pasture lands round about the cities' (Num. 35:2). 'Command the people of Israel and say to them, "My offering, my food for my offerings by fire, my pleasing odor you shall take heed to offer to me in its due season"' (Num. 28:2). Lo, we see in all these cases that the purpose of a commandment is solely to bring about the expenditure of money.

E. "There is one exception, and what is that? It is this verse: 'Command the people of Israel and say to them, "When you enter the land of Canaan, this is the land that shall fall to you for an inheritance, the land of Canaan in its full extent"' (Num. 34:2).

F. "You must give encouragement to them in the matter of the correct division of the land."

G. And Rabbi [Judah the Patriarch] says, "The use of the word 'commandment' in all passages serves only for the purpose of [3] imparting an admonition [not to do a given action], along the lines of the following: 'And the Lord God commanded the man, saying, "You may freely eat of every tree of the garden, but of the tree of the knowledge of good and evil you shall not eat"''' (Gen. 2:16).

A final instance of the same mode of thought—we now see that "paraphrase" is too modest a term for it—asks whether Scripture speaks of cases as such, or of cases as examples of the rule. And that question in general yields the answer, Scripture means to be exemplary, not specific. Not only so, but when we do generalize, as we shall in the following, the upshot will be to present a generalization entirely outside the framework of the passage under discussion.

I:V

1. A. "[The Lord said to Moses, 'Command the people of Israel] that they put out of the camp every leper and every one having a discharge, and every one that is unclean through contact with the dead'" (Num. 5:1-2).

    B. Why is the matter stated as it is? I know only that these three, that are enumerated, are subject to the law. How do I know that ostracism applies to all other unclean persons?

    C. R. Josiah would say, "You may construct an argument a fortiori. If unclean people are driven out of the camp that contains the ark, which is of lesser sanctity, all the more so should they be driven out of the camp of the Presence of God, which is of greater sanctity.

    D. "But if you were to propose reasoning on that basis, you would find yourself imposing a penalty merely on the basis of reason [and not on the basis of an explicit statement of Scripture, and one does not impose a penalty merely on the basis of reason].

E.   "That is why it is stated: '. . . they put out of the camp.'

F.   "Making that matter explicit in Scripture serves to teach you that penalties are not to be imposed merely on the basis of logic [but require explicit specification in Scripture]. [That is, Scripture made a point that reason could have reached, but Scripture made the matter explicit so as to articulate a penalty applicable for violating the rule.]"

I underscored in the preceding chapter that one of the initial, and precipitating, tasks of Midrash-compilation was to show the relationship between the Mishnah (and its companion, the Tosefta, a compilation of supplementary materials) and Scripture. Here is a case in which a passage of the Mishnah or the Tosefta is joined together with a verse of Scripture. Since very little secondary expansion is undertaken, we see that the main point is accomplished through the mere juxtaposition of one thing with something else. To me this is nothing more than a proof text joined to a passage of apodictic law deriving from the Mishnah or the Tosefta. I see no polemic, simply two statements of the law: the one as given in Scripture, the other as reframed in the Mishnah-mode. I give the passage of the Tosefta in boldface type.

I:IX

1.   A.   "[You shall put out both male and female, putting them outside the camp] that they may not defile their camp [in the midst of which I dwell]:"

       B.   On the basis of this verse, the rule has been formulated:

       C.   **There are three camps, the camp of Israel, the camp of the Levitical priests, and the camp of the Presence of God. From the gate of Jerusalem to the Temple mount is the camp of Israel, from the gate of the Temple mount to the Temple courtyard is the camp of the Levitical priesthood, and from the gate of the courtyard and inward is the camp of the Presence of God** [T. Kelim 1:12].

Amplification and paraphrase serve not only, or mainly, purposes of clarification of language, as in our opening cases, or of interpretation, as in the interest in generalization, or of relationship of one document to another, as in the case above. Even at the elementary level at which we now stand, we find a persistent inquiry of a theological order. For without theological standing as God's word, the Torah, whether written or oral, enjoys no privileged position, requires no sustained study, bears no message of consequence. Here is how, from a verse of Scripture, a fundamental theological position receives additional support. It tells us a principal concern of the exegete-theologians. It is to show that, even though Israel has sinned, Israel remains beloved by God. If I had to identify a single theological proposition that occupies the whole of the Midrash-compilations and precipitates a large proportion of Midrash-exegesis, it is that one view. All understand that the present situation of Israel, with the Temple in ruins and the sacrifices no longer offered, to signify that Israel has sinned. So what people want to know is whether, despite sin, God loves Israel. Keep in mind that even now, in the second or third century when this document was compiled, Christians read the same Scriptures, drew the same conclusions on the nature of history, and therefore asked the same question about Israel! And they answered the question in exactly the opposite way, finding in the destruction of the Temple evidence that God had now rejected Israel because of its sin, often claiming to form the new Israel that has been forgiven, in place of the old, unforgiven Israel after the flesh. So in perspective, what follows represents that urgent message, that personal message from God to me, that the Midrash-exegetes proposed to discover for themselves and their generation.

I:X

1. A. "[You shall put out both male and female, putting them outside the camp, that they may not defile their camp,] in the midst of which I dwell. [And the people of Israel did so and drove them outside the camp, as the Lord said to Moses, so the people of Israel did]" (Gen. 5:3-4).
   B. So beloved is Israel that even though they may become unclean, the Presence of God remains among them.
   C. And so Scripture states, ". . . who dwells with them in the midst of their uncleanness" (Lev. 16:16).
   D. And further: ". . . by making my sanctuary unclean, which [nonetheless] is in their midst " (Lev. 15:31).
   E. And it further says: ". . . that they may not defile their camp, in the midst of which I dwell" (Num. 5:3-4).
   F. And it further says, "You shall not defile the land in which you live, in the midst of which I dwell, for I the Lord dwell in the midst of the people of Israel" (Num. 35:34).
2. A. R. Yose the Galilean says, "Come and take note of how great is the power of sin. For before the people had laid hands on transgression, people afflicted with flux and lepers were not located among them, but after they had laid hands on transgression, people afflicted with flux and lepers did find a place among them.
   B. "Accordingly, we learn that these three events took place on one and the same day" [transgression, the presence of those afflicted with flux, the development of leprosy among the people].

3.   A.   R. Simeon b. Yohai says, "Come and take note of how great is the power of sin. For before the people had laid hands on transgression, what is stated in their regard?

     B.   "'Now the appearance of the glory of the Lord was like a devouring fire on the top of the mountain in the sight of the people of Israel' (Exod. 24:17).

     C.   "Nonetheless, the people did not fear nor were they afraid.

     D.   "But once they had laid hands on transgression, what is said in their regard?

     E.   "'And when Aaron and all the people of Israel saw Moses, behold, the skin of his face shone, and they were afraid to come near him'" (Exod. 34:30).

We take up a polemic: Israel is beloved, even though Israel sins. I:X.1 introduces the theological evaluation of the theme at hand, uncleanness. While Israelites are subject to uncleanness, that marks God's love for them: God loves them even though they may become unclean. That point is made by a series of facts: proof texts. Nothing, then, is particular to our passage. We have moved on to a general theme and expressed it as a syllogism proved by a list of facts. No. 2 goes on to another proposition independent of the present context but, of course, relevant to it. It is that uncleanness marks sin, and the fact that Israelites can become unclean indicates that they commit sin. Joined to no. 1, the larger proposition is powerful: while Israel sins, God still dwells among them. No. 3 completes the matter. Because of sin Israel loses its faith in God. The mark of regeneration, then, is their capacity to relate to God. The next passage pursues the same point, but in a different way.

I:XI

1.   A.   "[You shall put out both male and female, putting them outside the camp, that they may not defile their camp, in the midst of which I dwell.' And the people of Israel did so and drove them outside the camp, as the Lord said to Moses,] so the people of Israel did" (Gen. 5:3-4):

     B.   This statement [". . . And the people of Israel did so,"] serves to recount praise for the Israelites, for just as Moses instructed them, so did they do.

2.   A.   Scripture states, ". . . as the Lord said to Moses, so the people of Israel did."

     B.   What this teaches is that even the unclean people did not register opposition [but accepted the decree without complaint].

The proposition begun at I:X reaches a conclusion, in two further points. First, the Israelites obeyed God. Second, even the sinners among them, affected by uncleanness, submitted without complaint to God's will. I need hardly underscore the immediacy of the passage, how directly it addresses the everyday world of the people to whom it is offered as the Torah's message.

Sifré to Deuteronomy bears many of the same formal and exegetical traits as we have found in Sifré to Numbers. It too begins with a verse of Scripture, which is cited and then treated as occasion for some sort of secondary development: amplification, application, above all, generalization. If we wish to know how the sages of the dual Torah read in a sustained way an important passage of a legal character, one that instructed people not only what to believe but what they must do, the following sample of this great Midrash-compilation shows us. It is important for us to see not only the parts but the whole, for now we shall follow how, viewing a passage, the Midrash-compilers assembled materials to recast the whole within the framework that they wished to construct. The passage deals with the celebration of the harvest by consuming the produce, new grain, wine, oil, firstlings of the herds and the flocks, "before the Lord" in the Temple in Jerusalem. What we see is how details are patiently sifted and reframed into a much broader statement, so that, as we noted just now, the case of Scripture is turned into a rule that prevails in a variety of cases. That is one of the great accomplishments of the first stage in the making of Midrash-compilations, which is, as we realize, amplification, paraphrase, reframing and reconstruction. What quickly emerges is not merely a review of what Scripture says but a fundamental transformation of Scripture—details, rules, stories, admonitions—into Torah: a whole and harmonious world built on God's word. The word *pisqa*, with the plural *pisqaot*, stands for "chapter." Another word we shall see is *parashah*, with the plural *parashiyyot*, bearing the same sense.

Sifré to Deuteronomy *Pisqaot* Seventy-two and Seventy-three to Deuteronomy 12:13–19

LXXII:I

1. A. "You may not partake in your settlements [of the tithes of your new grain or wine or oil or of the firstlings of your herds and flocks or of any of the votive offerings that you vow, or of your freewill offerings or of your contributions. These you must consume before the Lord your God in the place that the Lord your God will choose—you and your sons and your daughters, your male and female slaves, and the Levite in your settlements—happy before the Lord your God in all your undertakings. Be sure not to neglect the Levite as long as you live in your land]" (Deut. 12:13–19):

B. R. Joshua b. Qorhah says, "[Since the verse at hand reads, 'you cannot eat it . . . ,'] in fact, I can do it, but I am not permitted to do it."

2. A. Along these same lines: "And as for the Jebusites, inhabitants of Jerusalem, the children of Judah could not drive them out" (Josh. 15:63).

B. They could have done it, but were not permitted to.

The basic proposition is clear, and the two instances of it provide the same insight into the distinction at hand.

LXXII:II

1. A. ". . . of the tithes [of your new grain or wine or oil or of the firstlings of your herds and flocks or of any of the votive offerings that you vow, or of your freewill offerings or of your contributions. These you must consume before the Lord your God in the place that the Lord your God will choose—you and your sons and your daughters, your male and female slaves, and the Levite in your settlements—happy before the Lord your God in all your undertakings. Be sure not to neglect the Levite as long as you live in your land]" (Deut. 12:13–19):

B. I know only that the rule applies to what is cultically clean. How do I know that it applies equally to the unclean?

C. Scripture says, ". . . of your new grain."

D. How do I know that it applies for what is purchased with money that is in the status of second tithe [and must be spent for food to be eaten in Jerusalem]?

E. Scripture says, ". . . your wine."

F. I know only that the rule applies to what is cultically clean. How do I know that it applies equally to the unclean?

G. Scripture says, ". . . of your oil."

2. A. R. Simeon says, "Since the verse states, 'I have not eaten of it when I was mourning, and I have not put any of it away when it was unclean' (Deut. 26:16), I do not know where is this indicated by way of admonition?

B. "Scripture states, 'You may not partake in your settlements of the tithes' [of your new grain or wine or oil or of the firstlings of your herds and flocks or of any of the votive offerings that you vow, or of your freewill offerings or of your contributions].'"

3. A. Might I suppose that one who gives it away is also liable [to the prohibition]?

B. Scripture states, "You may not partake in your settlements of the tithes [of your new grain or wine or oil or of the firstlings of your herds and flocks or of any of the votive offerings that you vow, or of your freewill offerings or of your contributions]."

C. One who eats it [when in mourning] is liable, but one who gives it away as a gift [under that circumstance] is not liable.

4. A. R. Yose the Galilean says, "I might suppose that people are liable on account only of totally untithed produce, from which no offerings have been removed of any kind.

    B. "How do I know that if the priestly ration has been removed from produce, but the first tithe has not been removed, the first tithe has been removed but not the second tithe, or even the poor man's tithe,

    C. "how under all of these circumstances is one liable?

    D. "Scripture states, 'You may not partake in your settlements of the tithes [of your new grain or wine or oil or of the firstlings of your herds and flocks or of any of the votive offerings that you vow, or of your freewill offerings or of your contributions].'"

5. A. R. Simeon says, "The purpose of the verse of Scripture is only to make distinctions among Lesser Holy Things."

6. A. "Nor your freewill offerings" ["the offering of your hand"]:

    B. this refers to first fruits.

    C. Now what precisely does this verse of Scripture serve to tell us? If it is that first fruits are not to be eaten outside the wall of Jerusalem, that rule derives from the one pertaining to tithe.

    D. Specifically, if tithe, which may be eaten by nonpriests, imposes liability for violating a negative commandment on anyone who eats it outside the wall of Jerusalem, first fruits, which are forbidden to nonpriests, surely should impose liability for violating a negative commandment on anyone who eats them outside the wall of Jerusalem.

    E. The purpose of the verse of Scripture is solely to tell you that one who consumes first fruits prior to their having been designated as such violates a negative commandment.

7. A. ". . . [of any of the votive offerings that you vow] or of your freewill offerings or of your contributions":

    B. This refers to the thank-offering and peace-offerings.

    C. Now what precisely does this verse of Scripture serve to tell us? If it is whether or not one may eat the meat of thank-offerings or peace-offerings outside the wall of Jerusalem, that prohibition in fact derives from the one governing tithe.

    D. Specifically, if one is liable for eating outside the wall of Jerusalem tithe, which is not subject to liability on the counts of allowing the meat to lie over, leaving remnants of the meat unconsumed, and eating the meat in a state of uncleanness, surely one should be liable for eating outside the wall of Jerusalem the meat of thank-offerings and peace-offerings, which is not subject to liability on the counts of allowing the meat to lie over, leaving remnants of the meat unconsumed, and eating the meat in a state of uncleanness.

    E. The purpose of the rule is solely to let you know that one who eats the meat of a thank-offering or peace-offerings prior to the tossing of the blood [on the corner of the altar] is liable for violating a negative commandment.

8. A. "Firstlings":
    B. this refers to a firstling.
    C. Now what precisely does this verse of Scripture serve to tell us? If it is whether or not one may eat the meat of thank-offerings or peace-offerings outside the wall of Jerusalem, that prohibition in fact derives from the one governing tithe;
    D. if it has to do with the rule governing eating the meat prior to the sprinkling of the blood, that derives from an argument a fortiori from the rule governing the thank-offering and peace-offerings.
    E. Specifically, if one is liable for eating prior to the sprinkling of the blood the thank-offering and peace-offerings, which are permitted for consumption by nonpriests, in the case of a firstling, which is forbidden for eating by nonpriests, surely one who eats the meat prior to the sprinkling of the blood should be liable.
    F. The purpose of the Scripture is solely to let you know that a nonpriest who ate the meat of a firstling, whether this was before the sprinkling of the blood or afterward, is liable for violating a negative commandment.

LXXIII:I

1. A. ". . . of the firstlings of your herds and flocks":
    B. This refers to the sin-offering and guilt-offering.
    C. Now what does Scripture propose to tell us? Is it whether or not one who eats the meat of a sin-offering or guilt-offering outside the wall of Jerusalem is liable? That fact derives from an argument a fortiori from the case of tithe.
    D. Is it whether or not one is liable who eats the meat prior to the sprinkling of the blood? That rule derives from an argument a fortiori based on the thank-offering and the peace-offering.
    E. Is it whether or not one is liable who eats the meat after the sprinkling of the blood? That rule derives from the one governing the firstling, specifically:
    F. if one who after the sprinkling of the blood eats the meat, the firstling, which is in the status of Lesser Holy Things, is liable on the count of violating a negative commandment, one who eats the meat of a sin-offering or guilt-offering, which are in the status of Most Holy Things, should surely be liable for violating a negative commandment.
    G. The purpose of the verse of Scripture is solely to let you know that one who eats the meat of a sin-offering or guilt-offering outside the hangings of the temple is liable for violating a negative commandment.

No. 1 accomplishes a systematic exegesis of the base verse, yielding the same point for its several components. No. 2 is not spelled out. No. 3 answers a question no one in our context has asked. Nos. 4 and 5 present yet another miscellany. But nos. 6, 7, and 8 form a remarkably cogent exercise, arguing time and again in a systematic way that the basic point at hand is self-evident, and, therefore, Scripture has another proposition in mind. This same systematic argument continues in a rather striking and substantial sustained statement. The construction follows the established pattern to make an important point.

The discussions in this chapter show us what it means to "apply" the Torah to "the everyday world." What is required is much more than mere free association between what I am thinking this minute and the passage of Scripture that I happen upon. What is involved is a sustained program, which we can reconstruct out of their treatment of Scripture, made up of systematic questions. The model allows us to form our own sustained program, made up of questions that we should address to any and every passage of our choice. That is what is meant by "applying the Torah to the everyday world": something orderly, systematic, purposeful, and disciplined. Order, discipline, and purpose, however, emerge from our perception of a world of order, marred by chaos, a world of rules, which are violated, and a world of purpose, which is full of aberrations and incomprehensible happenings.

5

Sifra

THE ISSUE OF THE RELATIONSHIP
OF SCRIPTURE'S CATEGORIES
TO OUR CATEGORIES

What we find in Sifra is nothing less than a solution to a long-standing problem in the theology, literature, and law of the Judaism of the Dual Torah. The problem was posed—so we already know—by the character and standing of the Mishnah. From the moment of its promulgation as the basis for the law of Judaism, the Mishnah was represented as authoritative, therefore, in the context of Israel's life, as enjoying the standing, or falling into the classification, of *torah*, divine revelation, yet clearly not like the Torah revealed by God to Moses at Sinai. There were two solutions to that problem, the one of the successor documents, particularly the Tosefta and the two Talmuds, that undertook the exegesis, amplification, and application of the Mishnah, the other presented by the authorship of Sifra. The solution to that problem worked out by the successor authorities to the Mishnah, in Tosefta, ca. A.D. 300, the Talmud of the Land of Israel or Yerushalmi, ca. A.D. 400, and the Talmud of Babylonia or Bavli, ca. A.D. 600, was to treat the word or conception, *torah*, as a common noun, signifying, among other things, process, status, or classification. Then the Mishnah found ample place for itself within the capacious classification, *torah*.

The solution to that problem worked out by the authorship of Sifra was to treat the word, *torah*, as solely a proper noun, the Torah, but *also* to insist that the Mishnah found a fully legitimate position within the Torah. That solution required the authorship of the Mishnah to undertake a profound and thoroughgoing critique of the logic of the Mishnah, both as that logic dictated the correct joining of two or more sentences into a cogent thought, and as that logic governed the formation of propositions for analysis. In fact, the authorship of Sifra set forth a systematic critique of the Mishnah in its principal definitive traits: its topical program and arrangement, its principles of cogent discourse, and its logic of critical analysis and probative demonstration of propositions. It furthermore set forth a sizable portion of the Mishnah's contents, as these pertained to the book of Leviticus, within its own definition of the correct topical program and arrangement, its own principles of cogent discourse, and its own logic of critical analysis and proof.

These two solutions came to full expression, one paramount in the several works of exegesis and amplification that adopted the Mishnah, the oral Torah, as the base text, the other in Sifra. Sifra's authorship explored profound issues of the fundamental and generative structure of right thought, yielding, as a matter of fact, both Scripture and the Mishnah. This approach insisted that *torah* always was a proper noun. There was, and is, only *the* Torah. But this—the Torah—demanded expansion and vast amplification. When we know the principles of logical structure and especially those of hierarchical classification that animate the Torah, we can undertake part of the task of expansion and amplification, that is, join in the processes of thought that, in the mind of God, yielded the Torah. For when we know how God thought in giving the Torah to Moses at Sinai and so accounting for the classifications and their ordering in the very creation of the world, we can ourselves enter into the Torah and participate in its processes.

The discussion was carried on on two fronts, negative and positive. The Sifra's authorship conducts a sustained polemic against the failure of the Mishnah to cite Scripture very much or systematically to link its ideas to Scripture through the medium of formal demonstration by exegesis. Sifra's rhetorical exegesis follows a standard redactional form. Scripture will be cited. Then a statement will be made about its meaning, or a statement of law correlative to that Scripture will be given. That statement sometimes cites the Mishnah, often verbatim. Finally, the author of Sifra invariably states, "Now is that not (merely) logical?" And the point of that statement will be, Can this position not be gained through the working of mere logic, based upon facts supplied (to be sure) by Scripture? And the answer is, always, No, no, never! The polemical power of Sifra lies in its repetitive demonstration that the stated position, citation of a Mishnah-pericope, is not only not the product of logic, but is, and only can be, the product of exegesis of Scripture. Sifra's writers carried to a much more profound level of thought the critique of the Mishnah. They did so by rethinking the logical foundations of the entire

Torah. And that forms the positive side of the Sifra's writers' theological Midrash-exegesis.

To understand how they accomplished that intellectual feat, let us briefly review the Mishnah's logic of cogent discourse, which establishes propositions that rest upon philosophical bases—for example, through the proposal of a thesis and the composition of a list of facts that prove the thesis. This—to us entirely familiar, Western—mode of scientific expression through the classification of data that, in a simple way, we may call the science of making lists (*Listenwissenschaft*) is exemplified by the Mishnah. The issue at hand is one of connection, that is, not of fact (such as is conveyed by the statement of the meaning of a verse or a clause of a verse) but of the relationship between one fact and another. That relationship—for example, connection—is shown in a conclusion, different from the established facts of two or more sentences, that we propose to draw when we set up as a sequence two or more facts and claim out of that sequence to propose a proposition different from, transcending, the facts at hand. We demonstrate propositions in a variety of ways, appealing to both a repertoire of probative facts and also a set of accepted modes of argument. In this way we engage in a kind of discourse that gains its logic from what, in general, we may call philosophy: the rigorous analysis and testing of propositions against the canons of an accepted reason.

The Mishnah's authorship appeals to the centrality of classification, the appeal of the logic of hierarchical classification in the demonstration of comparisons and contrasts, in the formation of the thought of the document. For sanctification in the Mishnah's system—and that is what the Mishnah's authorship wishes to explore—means establishing the stability, order, regularity, predictability, and reliability of Israel in the world of nature and supernature, in particular at moments and in contexts of danger. And it is through assigning to all things their rightful name, setting of all things in their proper position, that we discover the laws of stability, order, regularity, and predictability. Danger means instability, disorder, irregularity, uncertainty, and betrayal. Each topic of the system as a whole takes up a critical and indispensable moment or context of social being. Through what is said in regard to each of the Mishnah's principal topics, what the system as a whole wishes to declare is fully expressed. Yet if the parts severally and jointly give the message of the whole, the whole cannot exist without all of the parts, so well joined and carefully crafted are they all.

What this means for the requirements of logical demonstration is quite obvious. To show something to be true, one has to demonstrate that, in logic, it conforms to the regularity and order that form the guarantee of truth. Analysis is meant to discover order: the rule that covers diverse, by nature disorderly, things, the shared trait, the general and prevailing principle of regularity. And to discover the prevailing rule, one has to know how to classify things that seem to be each sui generis, how to find the rule that governs diverse things. And that explains the centrality in the system of the Mishnah of the classification of things. At issue between the framers of the Mishnah and the authorship of Sifra is the correct sources of classification. The framers of the Mishnah effect their taxonomy through the traits of things. The authorship of Sifra insists that the source of classification is Scripture. Sifra's authorship time and again demonstrates that classification without Scripture's data cannot be carried out without Scripture's data, and, it must follow, hierarchical arguments based on extrascriptural taxa always fail.

Let me now present a single sustained example of how Sifra's authorship rejects the principles of the logic of hierarchical classification *as these are worked out by the framers of the Mishnah*. I emphasize that the critique applies to the way in which a shared logic is worked out by the other authorship. For it is not the principle that like things follow the same rule, unlike things, the opposite rule, that is at stake. Nor is the principle of hierarchical classification embodied in the argument a fortiori at issue. What our authorship disputes is that we can classify things on our own by appeal to the traits or indicative characteristics, that is, utterly without reference to Scripture.

The argument is simple. On our own, we cannot classify species into genera. Everything is different from everything else in some way. But Scripture tells us what things are like what other things for what purposes; hence Scripture imposes on things the definitive classifications. That and not traits we discern in the things themselves. Because the Mishnah's authorship sets up its own classifications, not relying solely upon Scripture's, the nature of the critique is clear. We shall consider a complete chapter, rather than only a snippet; this allows us to follow the modes of exposition, as much as of argument, in this Midrash-compilation. The division is "Vayyiqra [=Leviticus] Dibura Denedabah" [the section on free-will offerings], the seventh parashah. My numbering scheme, which treats all passages as sequential, is superimposed; this is the fourteenth chapter of Sifra as a whole. Hence the double reference-system.

14. Sifra Parashat Vayyiqra Dibura Denedabah Parashah 7

XIV:I

1. A. ["If his offering to the Lord is a burnt offering of birds, he shall choose [bring near] his offering from turtledoves or pigeons. The priest shall bring it to the altar, pinch off its head, and turn it into smoke on the altar; and its blood shall be drained out against the side of the altar. He shall remove its crop with its contents and cast it into the place of the ashes, at the east side of the altar. The priest shall tear it open by its wings, without severing it, and turn it into smoke on the altar, upon the wood that is on the fire. It is a burnt offering, an offering by fire, of pleasing odor to the Lord" (Lev. 1:14–17)]:

    B. "[The priest] shall bring it [to the altar]":

    C. What is the sense of this statement?

    D. Since it is said that "he shall choose [bring near] his offering from turtledoves or pigeons," one might have supposed that there can be no fewer than two sets of birds.

    E. Accordingly, Scripture states, "[The priest] shall bring it [to the altar]" to indicate [by reference to the "it"] that even a single pair suffices.

Reduced to its simplest syntactic traits, the form consists of the citation of a clause of a verse, followed by secondary amplification of that clause. We may call this commentary form, in that the rhetorical requirement is citation plus amplification. Clearly, the form sustains a variety of expressions—for example, the one at hand: "what is the sense of this statement . . . since it is said . . . accordingly Scripture states. . . ." But for our purposes there is no need to differentiate within the commentary form.

2. A. "The priest shall bring it to the altar, pinch off its head":

    B. Why does Scripture say, "The priest . . . pinch off . . ."?

    C. This teaches that the act of pinching off the head should be done only by a priest.

    D. But is the contrary to that proposition not a matter of logic:

    E. if in the case of a beast of the flock, to which the act of slaughter at the north side of the altar is assigned, the participation of a priest in particular is not assigned, to the act of pinching the neck, to which the act of slaughter at the north side of the altar is not assigned, surely should not involve the participation of the priest in particular!

    F. That is why it is necessary for Scripture to say, "The priest . . . pinch off . . . ,"

    G. so as to teach that the act of pinching off the head should be done only by a priest.

3. A. Might one compose an argument to prove that one should pinch the neck by using a knife?

    B. For lo, it is a matter of logic.

    C. If to the act of slaughter [of a beast as a sacrifice], for which the participation of a priest is not required, the use of a correct utensil is required, for the act of pinching the neck, for which the participation of a priest indeed is required, surely should involve the requirement of using a correct implement!

    D. That is why it is necessary for Scripture to say, "The priest . . . pinch off . . . ."

4. A. Said R. Aqiba, "Now would it really enter anyone's mind that a nonpriest should present an offering on the altar?

    B. "Then why is it said, 'The priest . . . pinch off . . .'?

    C. "This teaches that the act of pinching the neck must be done by the priest using his own finger [and not a utensil]."

5. A. Might one suppose that the act of pinching may be done either at the head [up by the altar] or at the foot [on the pavement down below the altar]?

    B. It is a matter of logic:

    C. if in the case of an offering of a beast, which, when presented as a sin-offering is slaughtered above [at the altar itself] but when slaughtered as a burnt offering is killed below [at the pavement, below the altar], in the case of an offering of fowl, since when presented as a sin-offering it is slaughtered down below, surely in the case of a burnt offering it should be done down below as well!

    D. That is why it was necessary for Scripture to make explicit [that it is killed up by the altar itself]: "The priest shall bring it to the altar, pinch off its head, and turn it into smoke on the altar."

    E. The altar is explicitly noted with respect to turning the offering into smoke and also to pinching off the head.

    F. Just as the offering is turned into smoke up above, at the altar itself, so the pinching off of the head is to be done up above, at the altar itself.

The form at hand is to be characterized as a dialectical exegetical argument, in which we move from point to point in a protracted, yet very tight, exposition of a proposition. The proposition is both implicit and explicit. The implicit proposition is that "logic" does not suffice, a matter vastly spelled out in Uniting the Dual Torah. The explicit proposition concerns the subject matter at hand. We may identify the traits of this form very simply: citation of a verse or clause + a proposition that interprets that phrase, then "it is a matter of logic" followed by the demonstration that logic is insufficient for the determination of taxa.

XIV:II

1. A. ". . . pinch off its head":
   B. The pinching off of the head is done at the shoulder.
   C. Might one suppose that it may be done at any other location?
   D. It is a matter of logic. Lo, I shall argue as follows:
   E. here an act of pinching off the neck is stated, and elsewhere we find the same [Lev. 5:8: "He shall bring them to the priest, who shall offer first the one for the sin-offering, pinching its head at the nape without severing it"].
   F. Just as pinching off at the neck in that passage is to be done at the nape of the neck, so pinching off at the neck in the present context is to be done at the nape of the neck.
   G. Perhaps the analogy is to be drawn differently, specifically, just as the pinching stated in that other passage involves pinching the neck without dividing the bird [Lev. 5:8: "without severing it"], so the importance of the analogy is to yield the same rule here.
   H. In that case, the priest would pinch the neck without severing it.
   I. Accordingly [the ambiguous analogy is such as to require] Scripture to state, ". . . pinch off its head."

We have an example of the dialectical exegesis of the limitations of logic for definition of taxa.

2. A. "[Turn it into smoke on the altar;] and its blood shall be drained out":
   B. Can one describe matters in such a way?
   C. Specifically, after the carcass is turned into smoke, can one drain out the blood?
   D. But one pinches the neck in accord with the way in which one turns it into smoke:
   E. just as we find that the turning of the carcass into smoke is done up to the head by itself and then the body by itself, so in the act of pinching the neck, the head is by itself and the body is by itself.
3. A. And how do we know that in the case of turning a carcass into smoke, the head is done by itself?
   B. When Scripture says, "The priest [shall tear it open by its wings, without severing it,] and turn it into smoke on the altar" (Lev. 1:17),
   C. lo, the turning of the body into smoke is covered by that statement.
   D. Lo, when Scripture states here, "pinch off its head, and turn it into smoke on the altar," it can only mean that the head is to be turned into smoke by itself.
   E. Now, just as we find that the turning of the carcass into smoke is done up to the head by itself and then the body by itself, so in the act of pinching the neck, the head is by itself and the body is by itself.

Nos. 2 and 3 present in a rather developed statement the simple exegetical form. The formal requirement is not obscured, however for all we have is the citation of a clause followed by secondary amplification. This version of commentary form obviously cannot be seen as identical to the other; but so far as the dictates of rhetoric are concerned, there is no material difference, for the variations affect only the secondary amplification of the basic proposition, and in both cases, the basic proposition is set forth by the citation of the verse or clause followed by a sentence or two of amplification.

XIV:III

1. A. ". . . and its blood shall be drained out [against the side of the altar]":
   B. all its blood: he takes hold of the head and the body and drains the blood out of both pieces.
2. A. ". . . against the side of the altar":
   B. not on the wall of the ramp up to the altar, and not on the wall of the foundation, nor on the wall of the courtyard.
3. A. It is to be on the upper half of the wall.
   B. Might one suppose it may be on the lower half of the wall?
   C. It is a matter of logic: in the case of the sacrifice of a beast, which, if done as a sin-offering, has its blood tossed on the upper part of the wall, and if done as a burnt-offering, has its blood tossed on the lower part of the wall,
   D. in the case of the sacrifice of a bird, since, if it is offered as a sin-offering, the blood is tossed at the lower half of the wall, should logic not dictate that if it is offered as a burnt offering, its blood should be tossed on the lower part of the wall as well?
   E. That is why it is necessary for Scripture to frame matters in this way:
   F. "The priest shall bring it to the altar, pinch off its head, and turn it into smoke on the altar; and its blood shall be drained out against the side of the altar,"
   G. the altar is noted with respect to turning the carcass into smoke and also with reference to the draining of the blood.
   H. Just as the act of turning the carcass into smoke is done at the topside of the altar, so the draining of the blood is done at the topside of the altar.
4. A. How does the priest do it?
   B. **The priest went up on the ramp and went around the circuit. He came to the southeastern corner. He would wring off its head from its neck and divide the head from the body. And he drained off its blood onto the wall of the altar** [M. Zeb. 6:5B-E].
   C. **If one did it from the place at which he was standing and downward by a cubit, it is valid. R. Simeon and R. Yohanan ben Beroqah say,**

"The entire deed was done only at the top of the altar" [T. Zeb. 7:9C-D].

The passage before us shows us how the interest in amplification shapes the Midrash-exegesis. The materials are entirely familiar from those we saw in chapter 4. What we have at the end is the verbatim citation of a passage of the Mishnah or of the Tosefta, joined to its setting in the exegetical framework of Sifra by some sort of joining formula. Now comes a further exposition through amplification and paraphrase.

XIV:IV

1. A. "He shall remove its crop [with its contents and cast it into the place of the ashes, at the east side of the altar]":
   B. this refers to the bird's crop.
   C. Might one suppose that one should extract the crop with a knife and remove it surgically?
   D. Scripture says, "... with its contents."
   E. He should remove it with its contents [including the innards, or, alternatively, the feathers].
   F. Abba Yosé b. Hanan says, "He should remove the intestines with it."

A variation on commentary form, we have secondary development at C, might one suppose? I am not inclined to think a sizable catalogue of variations on commentary form will materially advance our inquiry.

The examplary chapter allows us to identify the forms of Sifra. A simple formal program, consisting of three types of forms, served for every statement in the illustrative material I have now surveyed. An author of a pericope could make use of one or more of three forms but of no other forms at all. They were commentary, dialectical, and citation forms. The commentary consisted of a phrase of Scripture followed by some words of amplification; the dialectical, the largest and most distinctive, involved a sustained argument, and the citation form provided for the verbatim citation of a passage of the Mishnah. On the basis merely of the formal characteristics of the document, we may furthermore say that these were, first, the demonstration that if we wish to classify things, we must follow the taxa dictated by Scripture rather than relying solely upon the traits of the things we wish to classify; and, second, the citation of passages of the Mishnah or the Tosefta in the setting of Scripture. The forms of the document admirably expressed the polemical purpose of the authorship at hand. What they wished to prove was that a taxonomy resting on the traits of things without reference to Scripture's classifications cannot serve. They further wished to restate the oral Torah in the setting of the written Torah. And, finally, they wished to accomplish the whole by rewriting the written Torah. The dialectical form accomplished the first purpose, the citation form the second, and the commentary form the third.

Now to the main point: What about the issue of the correct sources for classifying things? In the following passage, we shall see how the Mishnah's classifications, which are extrinsic to Scripture, are rejected, and those of Scripture are shown to be the only reliable means of classifying things and so discovering rules.

CLXIV:I

1. A. "And whoever sits on anything on which he who has the discharge has sat will be unclean [shall wash his clothes and bathe himself in water and be unclean until the evening]" (Lev. 15:6).
   B. I know only that this is the case if he sits on it and [actually] touches it. [That is to say, if the Zab is in direct contact with the chair, then he imparts uncleanness to it.]
   C. How do I know that [if the Zab sits on] ten chairs, one on the other, and even [if he sits] on top of a heavy stone [what is underneath is clean]? [If the chair bears the weight of the Zab, even though the Zab is not touching the chair, the chair is made unclean.]
   D. Scripture says, "And he who sits on the utensil on which the Zab has sat will be unclean"—
   E. In any place in which the Zab sits and imparts uncleanness, the clean person sits and becomes unclean.
   F. I know only that when the Zab sits on it, and the Zab is there [that it is unclean]. How do I know that I should treat the empty as the full one?
   G. Scripture says, "Utensil"—to treat the empty like the full.
   H. I know only that this [rule concerning transmission of the Zab's uncleanness merely through applying the burden of his weight, even without his actually being in contact with the object] applies to the chair. How do I know that it applies to the saddle?

Now we shift to the critique of classification based on hierarchical logic of taxonomy as is evidenced in the Mishnah:

   I. and it is logical:
   J. if we have found that Scripture does not distinguish between the one who carries and the one who is carried in respect to sitting, so we should not distinguish between the one who is carried and the one who carries with respect to the saddle.
   K. But what difference does it make to me that Scripture did not distinguish between carrying and being carried in respect to the chair?
   L. For it did not distinguish touching it and carrying it.
   M. Should we not distinguish between carrying and being carried with reference to the saddle,

N. for lo, it has indeed distinguished touching it from carrying it?
O. Scripture [accordingly is required] to state, "A "utensil"—to encompass even the saddle.

Here is a fine example of a mode of logic that establishes its fixed and formal character through repetition. When we see enough cases of what we have in hand, we realize that the logic of methodical analysis, asking the same question many times, does serve in Sifra to establish a profound sense of cogency and coherence among topically diverse discourses. The inclusionary method will utilize diverse rhetoric, but it always is characterized by the intent to encompass within a single law a variety of cases.

The intent is the same as that of the Mishnah, therefore, namely, to show the rule governing diverse cases. The contrary exercise, the one that excludes examples from a rule, is to be stipulated. That, of course, is also what the framers of the Mishnah propose through their making of lists of like and unlike things, and determination of the rule that governs them all. So when the framers of the Mishnah appeal to the making of lists, they do no more, and no less, than is accomplished by our authorship in its exegetical exercises of exclusion and inclusion. Here our authorship therefore demonstrates the possibility of doing through rewriting the written Torah precisely what the oral Torah is meant to do. The judgment on modes of cogent discourse operative in the Mishnah is tacitly negative; we do things this way because this is the way to do them, that is to say, through appeal to, and amplification of, the written Torah—not through appeal to, and ordering of, traits of things sorted out independently of the written Torah.

How do Scripture's categories relate to our categories—and what is at stake in the answer to that question? When we understand why the question is an urgent one, we will see how the theological crisis precipitated the hermeneutical program of Midrash-compilation. Not only so, but we shall see why Midrash-exegesis was essential to theological inquiry, a principle that will guide theological thought in our own time as well.

The authorship of Sifra concurs in the fundamental principle that sanctification consists in calling things by their rightful name, or, in philosophical language, discovering the classification of things and determining the rule that governs diverse things. Where that authorship differs from the view of the Mishnah concerns—I emphasize—*the origins of taxa*: how do we know what diverse things form a single classification of things. Taxa originate in Scripture. Accordingly, at stake in the critique of the Mishnah are not the principles of logic necessary for understanding the construction and inner structure of creation. All parties among sages concurred that the inner structure set forth by a logic of classification alone could sustain the system of ordering all things in proper place and under the proper rule. The like belongs with the like and conforms to the rule governing the like, the unlike goes over to the opposite and conforms to the opposite rule. When we make lists of the like, we also know the rule governing all the items on those lists, respectively. We know that and one other thing, namely, the opposite rule, governing all items sufficiently like to belong on those lists, but sufficiently unlike to be placed on other lists. That rigorously philosophical logic of analysis, comparison and contrast, served because it was the only logic that could serve a system that proposed to make the statement concerning order and right array.

We may state the upshot of Sifra's authorship's systemic discourse in a very simple way. Time and again Sifra's authorship demonstrates that the formation of classifications based on monothetic taxonomy, that is to say, traits that are not only common to both items but that are shared throughout both items subject to comparison and contrast, simply will not serve. For at every point at which someone alleges uniform, that is to say, monothetic likeness, Sifra's authorship will demonstrate difference. Then how to proceed? Appeal to some shared traits as a basis for classification: this is not like that, and that is not like this, but the indicative trait that both exhibit is such and so, that is to say, polythetic taxonomy. The self-evident problem in accepting differences among things and insisting, nonetheless, on their monomorphic character for purposes of comparison and contrast, cannot be set aside: who says? That is, if I can adduce in evidence for a shared classification of things only a few traits among many characteristic of each thing, then what stops me from treating all things alike?

Polythetic taxonomy opens the way to an unlimited exercise in finding what diverse things have in common and imposing, for that reason, one rule on everything. Then the very working of *Listenwissenschaft* as a tool of analysis, differentiation, comparison, contrast, and the descriptive determination of rules yields the opposite of what is desired. Chaos, not order, a mass of exceptions, no rules, a world of examples, each subject to its own regulation, instead of a world of order and proportion, composition and stability, will result.

That furthermore explains the appeal to Scripture, and, in our case, to Leviticus. God made the world. God through Adam called all things by their rightful names, placing each in its correct place in relationship to all others. We have the power to place all things into relationship with all others of the same genus because Scripture has endowed us with that power. The foundations of all scientific knowledge, achieved through the analytical processes of comparison and contrast, classification and differentiation, yielding the rule for the like, the opposite rule for the unlike, rest upon Scripture. That is why, quite by the way, the Mishnah cannot make its statement independent of Scripture—but can make its statement within the framework of Scripture.

We now see how, through the reform of practical reason, our authorship united the dual Torah and uncovered the single, uniform foundations for the multiform and polythetic realm of creation, inclusive of the celebration of creation in the cult that the book of Leviticus sets forth. Having said that, I may conclude with the obvious fact that only through attending to the book of Leviticus, read as the priestly authorship of the Priestly Code wanted it read, in relationship with Genesis 1:1–2:4, and no other book of the Pentateuch, can our authorship have made the point that it wished to make. It was, in an odd way, a generalization particular to its example. But the example encompassed the very structure of creation and the foundation of all nature—and supernature.

6

Mekhilta Attributed to R. Ishmael

THE ISSUE OF AMPLIFYING SCRIPTURE
BY ASSEMBLING AND SYSTEMATICALLY
SETTING FORTH ITS INFORMATION

Scripture not only covers a variety of topics. It also treats a given topic not all in one place but in various contexts. Accordingly, its categories are not the same as ours. One important task we must accomplish, if we are to derive from Scripture the information we require, is to reorganize for our own purposes scriptural truth. That involves not changing but paraphrasing, not interpreting but systematically assembling within our classifications facts that Scripture has portrayed in its system. That work is accomplished in the third of the three Midrash-compilations assigned to authorities of the period of the Mishnah itself. That is to say, all the sages quoted in the document at hand bear names that occur also in the Mishnah. Most scholarship assigns the compilation to that same period, that is, closure by ca. 200.

Mekhilta Attributed to R. Ishmael is the first scriptural encyclopaedia of Judaism. The work treats important parts of the book of Exodus, and I call it a scriptural encyclopaedia because its compilers have joined together expositions of topics, disquisitions on propositions, in general precipitated by the themes of scriptural narrative or the dictates of biblical law, and collects and arranges in accord with Scripture's order and program the exegeses—paraphrases or brief explanations—of clauses of biblical verses. The compilation therefore collects and arranges episodic observations on the sense or implications of Scripture. None of the other compilations of Midrash-exegeses—Sifré to Numbers, Sifré to Deuteronomy, Sifra, Genesis Rabbah, Leviticus Rabbah, Pesiqta deRab Kahana, Pesiqta Rabbati, and The Fathers According to Rabbi Nathan—exhibits the traits of a scriptural encyclopaedia. But

Midrash-compilations later on, through medieval and into modern times, are precisely that.

The other Midrash-compilations of ancient times generally make important points overall, not only in detail. We have already seen how Sifra and the two Sifrés do so. Each of the other compilations therefore constitutes an essentially autonomous statement of its own, making use of a distinctive rhetoric and logic to set forth a proposition particular to itself. Unlike Mekhilta Attributed to R. Ishmael, each one emerges as sharply differentiated and clearly defined through its distinctive viewpoint and particular polemic and also through its formal and aesthetic qualities. By contrast, in assembling conventions and banalities of the faith, this authorship has made a canonical statement.

In this context, "encyclopaedia" forms a metaphorical synonym for "canon," and Mekhilta Attributed to R. Ishmael emerges as a document that, *in itself*, bears canonical traits of theology and law. For a canon comprises separate books that all together make a single statement. In terms of the Judaism of the dual Torah, the canon is what takes scriptures of various kinds and diverse points of origin and turns scriptures into Torah, and commentaries on those scriptures into Torah as well, making them all into the one whole Torah—of Moses, our rabbi.

Now to the document seen in itself. A sustained address to approximately half of the book of Exodus, Mekhilta Attributed to R. Ishmael seen whole and in the aggregate presents a composite of three kinds of materials. The first is a set of ad hoc and episodic exegeses of some passages of Scripture. The second is a group of propositional and argumentative essays in exegetical form, in which theological principles are set forth and demonstrated. The third is a set of topical articles, some of them sustained, many of them well crafted, about important subjects of the Judaism of the dual Torah. Providing this encyclopaedia of information concerning theology and normative behavior has not required a sustained demonstration of a position, whether whole or even in part, distinctive to that authorship and distinct from positions set forth by other authorships.

This is indicated in two ways. First of all, our authorship has not composed an argument, prevailing through large tracts of the document, that is cogent in all details and accomplishes a main and overriding purpose. Sifra has already shown us how such an argument is set forth. Nor, second, has that authorship made a statement of important propositions through most of the information, whether topical or exegetical, that it lays out. That is not to suggest, however, that here we have a mere conglomerate of unrelated facts. Quite to the contrary, there is no understanding the facts before us without ample access to a complete system, which is to say, the system of the Judaism of the dual Torah of the canon of which our writing forms a principal part. Accordingly, the document before us participates in a system, but its authorship in no way proposes to shape or contribute to the setting forth of the system, other than by rehearsing a corpus of inert facts. To state matters very simply, if we want to know the shape and structure of the Judaism of the canon of the dual Torah, we find out here.

As usual, I provide in my selection access not only to the message but also to the medium, laying out what sages say in the way in which they say it. Hence I work my way through a line-by-line treatment of a biblical passage. My selection focuses upon the single most important passage in the written Torah, which is the Ten Commandments. Since both Judaism and Christianity identify the Ten Commandments as the most holy, the most authoritative, statement that God has given in the Torah/Old Testament, we do well to see how that statement emerges in an encyclopaedic form. Not only so, but, we now realize, Mekhilta Attributed to R. Ishmael shows us the Ten Commandments as the consensus of the Judaic sages, "our sages, of blessed memory," reads the Ten Commandments. So here, quite simply, is Judaism.

Mekhilta Attributed to R. Ishmael 51. Bahodesh 5

LI:I

1. A. "[And God spoke all these words, saying] 'I am the Lord your God [who brought you out of the land of Egypt, out of the house of bondage]'":

   B. Why were the Ten Commandments not stated at the very beginning of the Torah?

   C. The matter may be compared to the case of a king who came into a city. He said to the people, "May I rule over you?"

   D. They said to him, "Have you done us any good, that you should rule over us?"

   E. What did he then do? He built a wall for them, brought water for them, fought their battles.

   F. Then he said to them, "May I rule over you?"

   G. They said to him, "Yes, indeed."

   H. So the Omnipresent brought the Israelites out of Egypt, divided the sea for them, brought manna down for them, brought up the well for them, provided the quail for them, made war for them against Amalek.

   I. Then he said to them, "May I rule over you?"

   J. They said to him, "Yes, indeed."

2. A. Rabbi says, "This serves to express the praise that is coming to the Israelites.

   B. "For when all of them stood before Mount Sinai to receive the Torah, they were unanimous in receiving the dominion of God with a whole heart.

   C. "And not only so, but they exacted pledges for one another."

3. A. And it was not only what was overt alone that the Holy One, blessed be he, revealed himself to them to make a covenant with them,

   B. but also over what is done in secret:

   C. "the secret things belong to the Lord our God, and the things that are revealed" (Deut. 29:28).

   D. They said to him, "Concerning what is done openly we make a covenant with you, but we shall not make a covenant with you concerning what is done in secret,

   E. "so that one of us may not commit a sin in secret and the entire community [Lauterbach:] be held responsible for it."

4. A. "I am the Lord your God":

   B. Why is this stated? Since when he appeared at the sea, it was in the form of a mighty soldier making war, as it is said, "The Lord is a man of war" (Exod. 15:3),

   C. and when he appeared to them at Sinai, it was as an elder, full of mercy, as it is said, "And they saw the God of Israel" (Exod. 24:10),

   D. and when they were redeemed, what does Scripture say? "And the like of the very heaven for clearness" (Exod. 24:10); "I beheld until thrones were placed and one that was ancient of days sat" (Dan. 7:9); "A fiery stream issued" (Dan. 7:10)—

   E. [so God took on many forms]. It was, therefore, not to provide the nations of the world with an occasion to claim that there are two dominions in heaven,

   F. that Scripture says, "I am the Lord your God [who brought you up out of the land of Egypt, out of the house of bondage]":

   G. [This then bears the message:] "I am the one in Egypt, I am the one at the sea, I am the one at Sinai; I am the one in the past and I am the one in the age to come, the one in this age is the one in the world to come: "See now that I, even I, am he" (Deut. 32:39); "Even to old age I am the same" (Isa. 46:4); "Thus says the Lord, the king of Israel and his redeemer, the Lord of hosts: 'I am the first and I am the last'" (Isa. 44:6); "Who has wrought and done it? He who called the generations from the beginning. I the Lord who am the first and with the last I am the same" (Isa. 41:4).

5. A. R. Nathan says, "In this connection we find a refutation of the *minim* [people within the sages' ambience] who maintain that there are two dominions.

   B. "When the Holy One, blessed be he, went and said, 'I am the Lord your God [who brought you out of the land of Egypt, out of the house of bondage],' who went and opposed him?

C. "If you maintain that it was in secret that the matter was carried out, is it not said, 'I have not spoken in secret' (Isa. 45:19), 'I did not say to the children of Jacob' (Isa. 45:19), that to these only will I give it.

D. "'They sought me in the desert' (Isa. 45:19): did I not give it in public? And so too: 'I the Lord speak righteousness, I declare things that are right'" (Isa. 45:19).

6. A. Another interpretation of the verse, "[And God spoke all these words, saying,] 'I am the Lord your God [who brought you out of the land of Egypt, out of the house of bondage]'":

B. When the Holy One, blessed be he, went and said, "I am the Lord your God [who brought you out of the land of Egypt, out of the house of bondage],"

C. the mountains shook and the hills quavered, Tabor moved from Beth Elim and Carmel from Aspamia: "[Lauterbach:] As I live, says the king whose name is the Lord of hosts, surely as Tabor among the mountains and Carmel by the sea would come" (Jer. 46:18).

D. "This one was saying, 'I was called,' and that one was saying, 'I was called.'"

E. But when they heard from his mouth, "Who brought you out of the land of Egypt," each one stood still in place, saying, "He is dealing only with the one whom he brought forth from Egypt."

7. A. Another interpretation of the verse, "[And God spoke all these words, saying] 'I am the Lord your God [who brought you out of the land of Egypt, out of the house of bondage]'":

B. When the Holy One, blessed be he, went and said, "I am the Lord your God [who brought you out of the land of Egypt, out of the house of bondage]," the earth shook, as it is said, "Lord, when you went forth out of Seir, when you marched out of the field of Edom, the earth trembled" (Judges 5:4); "The mountains quaked at the presence of the Lord" (Judges 5:5); "The voice of the Lord is upon the waters . . . The voice of the Lord is mighty" (Ps. 29:3-4); "and in his palace, everyone says glory" (Ps. 29:9).

C. Their palaces were filled with the splendor of the Presence of God. At that time all the nations of the world collected around the wicked Balaam and said to him, "Balaam, perhaps the Omnipresent is going to destroy his world with a flood?"

D. He said to them, "Fools, the Holy One, blessed be he, has taken an oath to Noah that he will not bring a flood into the world, for it is said, 'For this is as the waters of Noah to me; for as I have sworn that the waters of Noah shall no more go over the earth . . .'" (Isa. 54:9).

E. They said, "Perhaps he will not bring a flood of water, but he may bring a flood of fire?"

F. He said to them, "He is going to bring neither a flood of water nor a flood of fire. It is Torah that the Holy One, blessed be he, is giving to his people: 'The Lord is giving strength to his people'" (Ps. 29:11).

G. When they had heard that from his mouth, they all turned around and each one went to his place.

8. A. Therefore the nations of the world were approached [to accept the Torah], so as not to give them an excuse to say, "If we had been approached, we should have accepted responsibility [for carrying out the Torah]."

B. Lo, they were approached but did not accept responsibility for them, as it is said, "The Lord came from Sinai" (Deut. 33:2).

9. A. ["The Lord came from Sinai" (Deut. 33:2)]:

B. [When the Omnipresent appeared to give the Torah to Israel, it was not to Israel alone that he revealed himself but to every nation.]

C. First of all he came to the children of the wicked Esau. He said to them, "Will you accept the Torah?"

D. They said to him, "What is written in it?"

E. He said to them, "'You shall not murder'" (Exod. 20:13).

F. They said to him, "The very being of 'those men' [namely, us] and of their father is to murder, for it is said, 'But the hands are the hands of Esau'(Gen. 27:22). 'By your sword you shall live'" (Gen. 27:40).

G. So he went to the children of Ammon and Moab and said to them, "Will you accept the Torah?"

H. They said to him, "What is written in it?"

I. He said to them, "'You shall not commit adultery'" (Exod. 20:13).

J. They said to him, "[The very essence of fornication belongs to them (us)], all of us are the children of fornication, for it is said, 'Thus were both the daughters of Lot with child by their fathers'" (Gen. 19:36).

K. So he went to the children of Ishmael and said to them, "Will you accept the Torah?"

L. They said to him, "What is written in it?"

M. He said to them, "'You shall not steal'" (Exod. 20:13).

N. They said to him, "This is the blessing that was stated to our father: 'And he shall be a wild ass of a man' (Gen. 16:12). 'For indeed I was stolen away out of the land of the Hebrews'" (Gen. 40:15).

O. But when he came to the Israelites: "At his right hand was a fiery law for them" (Deut. 33:2).

P. They all opened their mouths and said, "All that the Lord has spoke we shall do and we shall hear" (Exod. 24:7).

Q. "He stood and measured the earth, he beheld and drove asunder the nations" (Hab. 3:6).

10. A. R. Simeon b. Eleazar says, "If the seven religious duties that were assigned to the children of Noah they could not uphold, how much the more so all the religious duties that are in the Torah!

B.   "The matter may be compared to the case of a king who set up two administrators, one in charge of the supply of straw, the other in charge of the supply of silver and gold.

C.   "The one in charge of the supply of straw was suspected of thievery, and he complained that he had not been appointed over the supply of silver and gold.

D.   "They said to him, 'Fool! If you have been suspected of stealing from the straw supply, how are people going to entrust to you charge of the supply of silver and gold!'

E.   "Now this yields an argument a fortiori:

F.   "If the seven religious duties that were assigned to the children of Noah they could not uphold, how much the more so all the religious duties that are in the Torah!"

12. A.   Why was the Torah not given in the land of Israel?

B.   It was so as not to give an excuse to the nations of the world to say, "It is because the Torah was given in their land, therefore we did not accept responsibility for it upon ourselves."

13. A.   Another teaching concerning the question, [Why was the Torah not given in the land of Israel?]

B.   It was so as not to cause strife among the tribes, so that this one should not say, "In my territory the Torah was given," and that one should not say, "In my territory the Torah was given."

C.   Therefore it was given in the wilderness, in public, in the open, in territory that had no legal owner.

14. A.   To three things the Torah is compared: wilderness, fire, and water,

B.   so as to say to you, just as these are there for nothing, for everyone in the world,

C.   so teachings of the Torah are there for nothing, for everyone in the world.

15. A.   "Who brought you out of the land of Egypt, out of the house of bondage?"

B.   They were slaves to kings.

C.   You say that they were slaves to kings. But perhaps they were only slaves to slaves?

D.   When Scripture says, "And redeemed you out of the house of bondage, from the hand of Pharaoh, king of Egypt" (Deut. 7:8), [we see that] they were slaves to kings, not slaves to slaves.

16. A.   Another teaching concerning the clause, "who brought you out of the land of Egypt, out of the house of bondage":

B.   out of the house of those who worshiped, for they worshiped idolatry.

The exposition works on themes and propositions, rather than brief clauses. We see this right at the outset, no. 1, which makes a point, rather than paraphrasing what is at hand. Nos. 2 and 3 then go over yet another proposition, this time that the Israelites deserve praise for accepting the Torah, and that proposition continues in one form or another throughout,—for example, nos. 11 and 12, why Israel, not the nations of the world; why in the wilderness, and the like. Since our materials are not particular to the verse at hand, we cannot be surprised to find, materials of two kinds, first, those dealing with general propositions,—for example, no. 5, and, second, materials that occur elsewhere,—for example, nos. 4, 7, 8 and 9. As a composition, therefore, the present passage is readily distinguished from the others in context. The framer of this composition had in mind a different editorial purpose from those responsible for the composites made up entirely or mostly of brief citation and paraphrase.

Mekhilta Attributed to R. Ishmael 52. Bahodesh 6

LII:I

1. A. "You shall have no other gods before me" (Exod. 20:3):
   B. Why is this stated?
   C. Since it says, "I am the Lord your God."
   D. The matter may be compared to the case of a mortal king who came to a town. His staff said to him, "Issue decrees for them."
   E. He said to them, "No. When they accept my dominion, then I shall issue decrees over them. For if they do not accept my dominion, how are they going to carry out my decrees?"
   F. So said the Omnipresent to Israel, "I am the Lord your God.
   G. "You shall have no other gods before me.
   H. "I am the one whose dominion you accepted upon yourselves in Egypt."
   I. They said to him, "Indeed so."
   J. "And just as you accepted my dominion upon yourself, now accept my decrees: 'You shall have no other gods before me.'"

2. A. ["The Lord spoke to Moses saying, 'Speak to the Israelite people and say to them, I am the Lord your God'" (Lev. 18:2).]
   B. R. Simeon b. Yohai says, "That is in line with what is said elsewhere: 'I am the Lord your God [who brought you out of the land of Egypt, out of the house of bondage]' (Exod. 20:2).
   C. "'Am I the Lord, whose sovereignty you took upon yourself in Sinai?'
   D. "They said to him, 'Indeed.'
   E. "'And just as you accepted my dominion upon yourself, now accept my decrees.'
   F. "'You shall not copy the practices of the land of Egypt where you dwelt, or of the land of Canaan to which I am taking you; nor shall you follow their laws.'

G. "What is said here? 'I am the Lord your God [who brought you out of the land of Egypt, out of the house of bondage]' (Exod. 20:2).
H. "'Am I the Lord, whose sovereignty you took upon yourself?'
I. "They said to him, 'Indeed.'
J. "'And just as you accepted my dominion upon yourself, now accept my decrees.'
K. "You shall have no other gods before me" (Exod. 20:3).
3. A. "You shall have [no other gods before me]" (Exod. 20:3):
B. Why is this stated?
C. Because it is said, "You shall not make for yourself a graven image [or any likeness of anything that is in heaven above, or that is in the earth beneath, or that is in the water under the earth; you shall not bow down to them or serve them]."
D. I know only that one may not make them. How do I know that as to one that is already made, one may not keep it?
E. Scripture says, "You shall have [no other gods before me]" (Exod. 20:3).
4. A. "Other gods":
B. Are they gods at all? Has it not already been stated, "And have cast their gods into the fire; for they were no gods, but the work of men's hands, wood and stone, therefore they have destroyed them" (Isa. 37:19).
C. Why are they called "other gods" then?
D. It is because others call them gods.
5. A. Another comment on "other gods":
B. They are gods that hold back.
C. For they postpone [using the same letters as the word for "other"] goodness from coming into the world.
6. A. Another comment on "other gods":
B. For they make those who worship them into other [strangers to the true God].
7. A. Another comment on "other gods":
B. They act like others toward those who serve them.
C. And so Scripture says, "Yes, though one cries to him, he cannot answer, nor save him out of his trouble" (Isa. 46:7).
8. A. R. Yosé says, "Why are they called 'other gods'?
B. "So as not to give an opportunity for people to say, 'If they are called by his [God's] name, they would serve a need.' Lo, they are called by his name, but they serve no good purpose."
9. A. When were they called by his name?
B. In the time of Enosh, son of Seth. For it is said, "Then men began to call idols by the name of the Lord" (Gen. 4:26).
C. Then the ocean went and covered a third of the world.
D. Said to them the Holy One, blessed be He, "You have done a new

thing on your own initiative in calling [idols by my name]. So I too shall do a new thing and on my own initiative I shall call [the ocean]."

E. So it is said, "Who calls for the waters of the sea and pours them out upon the face of the earth, the Lord is his name" (Amos 5:8).

10. A. R. Eliezer says, "Why are they called 'other gods'?

B. "For every day they make for themselves new gods.

C. "How so? If one of them was of gold and the owner needs it, he makes it in silver instead; if it was in silver, he makes it over in copper; if it was copper, he makes it over in iron; if it was iron, he makes it over in tin; if it was tin and the owner needs it, he makes it over in lead; if it was lead and the owner needs it, he makes it over in wood.

D. "So it is said, 'New gods that came newly up'" (Deut. 32:17).

11. A. R. Isaac says, "Were the name of each idol to be made explicit, all of the parchments in the world would not suffice for them."

12. A. R. Hanina b. Antigonus says, "Go and see the language used by the Torah:

B. "'Molekh' 'to a ruler' (Lev. 18:21)—[that applies to] anything which you accept as a king over yourself, even a chip of wood or a piece of potsherd."

13. A. Rabbi says, "Why are they called 'other gods'?

B. "Because they are still later than the last among the creatures that were created.

C. "And they are called god by the one who was last in the process of creation [namely, man]."

14. A. "Before me":

B. Why is this stated?

C. So as not to give an excuse to the Israelites to say, "Only those who actually went forth from Egypt have been commanded concerning idolatry."

D. Therefore "before me" is stated, to indicate, just as I live and endure for ever and for all eternity, so you, your children, and your grandchildren shall not worship idols, to the end of all generations.

We have two different styles at hand, the systematic answer to the question of why they are called "gods" at all, nos. 4–13, and the "why is this stated" approach, nos. 1 and 14. The former shows us a different theory of composition, namely, assembling a large number of answers to a single question, precipitated to be sure by a verse of Scripture. We are a long way from the sustained and systematic glossing of successive clauses. That is simply not an approach taken here.

LII:II

1. A. "'You shall not make for yourself a graven image'":

B. One shall not make one that is engraved, but may one make one that is solid?

C. Scripture says, "or any likeness of anything."
D. One should not make a solid one, but may one plant a tree for oneself as an idol?
E. Scripture says, "You shall not plant an Asherah for yourself" (Deut. 16:21).
F. One may not plant a tree for oneself as an idol, but perhaps one may make a tree into an idol?
G. Scripture says, "of any kind of tree."
H. One may not make an idol of a tree, but perhaps one may make one of a stone?
I. Scripture says, "Nor shall you place any figured stone."
J. One may not make an idol of stone, but perhaps one may make an idol of silver or gold?
K. Scripture says, "Gods of silver or gods of gold you shall not make for yourself."
L. One may not make an idol of silver or gold, but perhaps one may make one of copper, iron, tin, or lead?
M. Scripture says, "Nor make for yourselves molten gods" (Lev. 19:4).
N. One may not make for oneself any of these images.
O. But may one make an image of any figure?
P. Scripture says, "Lest you deal corruptly and make for yourself a graven image, even the form of any figure" (Deut. 4:16).
Q. One may not make an image of a figure, but perhaps one may make an image of cattle or fowl?
R. Scripture says, "The likeness of any beast that is on the earth, the likeness of any winged fowl" (Deut. 4:17).
S. One may not make an image of cattle or fowl, but perhaps one may make an image of fish, locusts, unclean animals, or reptiles?
T. Scripture says, "The likeness of any thing that creeps on the ground, the likeness of any fish that is in the water" (Deut. 4:18).
U. One shall not make an image of any of these, but perhaps one may make an image of the sun, moon, stars, or planets?
V. Scripture says, "Lest you lift up your eyes to heaven" (Deut. 4:18).
W. One may not make an image of any of these, but perhaps one may make an image of angels, cherubim, or Ophannim?
X. Scripture says, "of anything that is in heaven."
Y. Since Scripture says, "that is in heaven above [or that is in the earth beneath, or that is in the water under the earth]," might one suppose that that involves only sun, moon, stars, or planets?
Z. It says, "above," that is, not the image of angels, cherubim, or Ophannim.
AA. One may not make an image of any of these, but perhaps one may make an image of deeps and darkness?
BB. Scripture says, "or that is in the water under the earth."

2.   A.   ["That is in heaven above, or that is in the earth beneath, or that is in
            the water under the earth."]
      B.   "This encompasses an image in a mirror," the words of R. Aqiba.
      C.   And some say, "It encompasses the *Shabrire*."
      D.   That is the extent to which Scripture pursued the impulse to do evil,
            so as not to give any pretext whatsoever to permitting [idolatry].
3.   A.   "You shall not bow down to them or serve them":
      B.   Why is this stated?
      C.   Because Scripture says, "and has gone and served other gods" (Deut.
            17:3).
      D.   That serves to impose liability for the act of worship by itself and for
            the act of prostration by itself.
      E.   That is what you say, but perhaps it means that one is guilty only if
            one has both performed an act of labor and also prostrated himself?
      F.   Scripture says, "you shall not bow down to them or serve them."
      G.   That serves to impose liability for the act of worship by itself and for
            the act of prostration by itself.
4.   A.   Another interpretation of the phrase, "you shall not bow down to
            them [or serve them]":
      B.   Why is this stated?
      C.   Because Scripture says, "He who sacrifices to gods other than the
            Lord shall be utterly destroyed" (Exod. 22:19).
      D.   Thus we derive the penalty, but what about the admonition?
      E.   Here it says, "you shall not bow down to them [or serve them]," and
            further: "you shall not bow down to any other god" (Exod. 34:14).
5.   A.   "For I the Lord your God am a jealous God":
      B.   Rabbi says, "God in charge of jealousy: 'I rule jealousy, but jealousy
            does not rule me.'
      C.   "'I rule sleep, but sleep does not rule me.'
      D.   "So Scripture says, 'Behold, he who keeps Israel neither slumbers nor
            sleeps'" (Ps. 121:4).
6.   A.   Another comment concerning "for I the Lord your God am a jealous
            God":
      B.   "It is with jealousy that I exact punishment from idolatry.
      C.   "But as to other matters, 'showing steadfast love.'"
7.   A.   A philosopher asked Rabban Gamaliel, "It is written in your Torah,
            'for I the Lord your God am a jealous God.'
      B.   "Now does an idol have any power to arouse jealousy against itself? A
            great athlete is jealous of another athlete, a sage is jealous of another
            sage, a rich man is jealous of another rich man. Then does an idol
            have any power to arouse jealousy against itself?"
      C.   He said to him, "If someone calls his dog by his father's name, so that,
            when he takes a vow, it is by the life of this dog, against whom will the
            father feel jealousy? The son or the dog?"

D.   He said to him, "There is some value in some of them."

E.   He said to him, "What evidence do you have?"

F.   He said to him, "Lo, there was a wild fire in a certain town, but the temple of idolatry of that town was saved. Did idolatry not stand up for itself?"

G.   He said to him, "Let me give you a parable. To what is the matter to be compared? To the case of a mortal king who goes out to make war. With whom does he make war? With the living or the dead?"

H.   He said to him, "With the living."

I.   He said to him, "If there is no value in any one of them, why does he not simply wipe it all out?"

J.   He said to him, "Now is it only one thing that you people worship? Lo, you worship the sun and the moon, the stars and the planets, the mountains and hills, springs and glens, and even man. Is he then going to destroy his entire world on account of idiots? 'Shall I utterly consume all things from off the face of the earth, says the Lord'" (Zeph. 1:2).

K.   [With reference to "and stumbling blocks with the wicked" (Zeph. 1:3)], he said to him, "Since the wicked stumble therein, why does he not remove it from the world?"

L.   He said to him, "On account of fowls? If so, they also worship man: 'Shall I cut off man from off the face of the earth'" (Zeph. 1:3).

8.   A.   "Visiting the iniquity of the fathers upon the children":

B.   That is when there is no break in the chain, but not when there is a break in the chain.

C.   How so?

D.   In the case of a wicked person, son of a wicked person, son of a wicked person.

E.   R. Nathan says, "It is one who cuts down [the plantings], son of one who cuts down [the plantings], son of one who cuts down [the plantings]."

F.   When Moses heard this matter, "Moses made haste and bowed his head toward the earth and worshiped" (Exod. 34:8).

G.   He said, "God forbid, there cannot be among all the Israelites a wicked person, son of a wicked person, son of a wicked person."

9.   A.   Might one suppose that, just as the measure of punishment covers four generations, so the measure of goodness covers the same span of four generations?

B.   Scripture says, "to thousands."

C.   If "to thousands," might I understand that the minimum plural of "thousands" is two?

D.   Scripture says, "to a thousand generations" (Deut. 7:9), that is to say, to generations beyond all discovering and all counting.

10.   A.   "Those who love me and keep my commandments":

B.   "those who love me" refers to Abraham, our patriarch, and those who are like him,

C.   "and who keep my commandments" refers to the prophets and elders.

11. A.   R. Nathan says, "'those who love me and keep my commandments' refers to those who dwell in the land of Israel and give their lives for keeping the religious duties.

B.   "'Why are you going forth to be put to death?' 'Because I circumcised my son as an Israelite.'

C.   "'Why are you going forth to be burned to death?' 'Because I read in the Torah.'

D.   "'Why are you going forth to be crucified?' 'Because I ate unleavened bread.'

E.   "'Why are you going to be given a hundred lashes?' 'Because I took up the palm branch [on Tabernacles].'

F.   "'Those with which I was wounded in the house of friends' (Zech. 13:6): these are the wounds that made me beloved to my father who is in heaven."

The protracted exposition, no. 1, follows a variety of possibilities; it is inserted here because our base text serves as one of the repertoire of proof texts; there is no particular proposition nor any close connection to our passage. No. 2 is tacked on, and the whole is given a suitable finis at 2.D, an unusual artifice. Nos. 3 and 4 go off in their own direction, each particular to the base verse but neither related to the other. No. 5 is again not made up to serve our verse, as 5.C shows. No. 7 introduces the colloquy on the theme of God's jealousy, which finds a natural place here, even though the base verse is not an important precipitant in making up the composition as a whole. We can well understand, at any rate, why a compiler would include the passage. No. 8 shows us what a comment particular to a component of the base verse looks like; it is possible only in response to the particular wording before us. Nos. 9 and 10 follow suit, and no. 11 is tacked on for its own reasons.

Mekhilta Attributed to R. Ishmael 53. Bahodesh 7

LIII:II

1. A.   "Remember the Sabbath day to keep it holy":

B.   "Remember" and "Keep" [at Deut. 5:12: "Keep the Sabbath day to keep it holy"] were both part of a single act of speech.

2. A.   "Everyone who profanes it shall surely be put to death" (Exod. 31:14),

B.   and "And on the Sabbath day two he-lambs" (Num. 28:9) were both part of a single act of speech.

3. A.   "You shall not uncover the nakedness of your brother's wife" (Lev. 18:16),

B. and "Her husband's brother shall go in to her" (Deut. 25:5) were both part of a single act of speech.

4. A. "You shall not wear a mingled stuff" (Deut. 22:11) and "You shall make yourself twisted cords" (Deut. 22:12) were both part of a single act of speech.

5. A. For it is said, "God has spoken once, but we have heard two things" (Ps. 62:12).

   B. And, "Is not my word like fire, says the Lord, and like a hammer that breaks the rock into pieces?" (Jer. 23:29).

6. A. "Remember" and "Keep":

   B. "Remember" in advance, and "keep" afterward.

   C. In this connection sages have said, "They add time from an ordinary day to a holy day."

   D. It is like a wolf who moves backward and forward.

7. A. Eleazar b. Hananiah b. Hezekiah b. Garon says, "'Remember the Sabbath day to keep it holy:'

   B. "you should remember it from Sunday, so that if something nice comes to hand, you should set it aside for the sake of the Sabbath."

   C. R. Isaac says, "You should not count the days of the week the way others do, but rather, you should count for the sake of the Sabbath [the first day, the second day, upward to the seventh which is the Sabbath]."

8. A. "[Remember the Sabbath day] to keep it holy":

   B. to keep it holy by reciting a blessing.

   C. In this connection sages have said, "They recite a prayer of sanctification over wine when the Sabbath enters."

   D. I know only that there is a prayer of sanctification recited by day. How do I know that there is a prayer of sanctification recited by night?

   E. Scripture says, "You shall keep the Sabbath" (Exod. 31:14).

   F. I know only that there is a prayer of sanctification for the Sabbath. How about festival days?

   G. Scripture says, "These are the appointed seasons of the Lord" (Lev. 23:4).

9. A. "Six days you shall labor and do all your work":

   B. But can a mortal carry out all of one's work in only six days?

   C. But the nature of Sabbath rest is such that it should be as though all of your labor has been carried out.

10. A. Another teaching [as to "Six days you shall labor and do all your work"]:

    B. "Take a Sabbath rest from the very thought of work."

    C. And so Scripture says, "If you turn away your foot because of the Sabbath" (Isa. 58:13), and then, "Then you shall delight yourself in the Lord" (Isa. 58:14).

11. A. "But the seventh day is a sabbath to the Lord your God":

B. Why is this stated?

C. Since Scripture says, "Whoever does any work on the Sabbath day shall surely be put to death" (Exod. 31:15), we are told the penalty, but not the admonition.

D. Accordingly, Scripture states, "but the seventh day is a sabbath to the Lord your God."

12. A. "In it you shall not do any work":

B. "I know therefore the penalty and admonition concerning work by day. Whence the penalty and admonition concerning work by night?

C. "Scripture says, 'Whoever does any work on the Sabbath day shall surely be put to death' (Exod. 31:15), we are told the penalty, but not the admonition.

D. "Accordingly, Scripture states, 'but the seventh day is a sabbath to the Lord your God.'

E. "For why should Scripture specify 'the Sabbath'? It is only to encompass the night within the classification of the admonition," the words of R. Ahai b. R. Josiah.

13. A. "You, or your son or your daughter":

B. This refers to minors.

C. Perhaps reference is made to the adults?

D. State matters as follows: are the adults not admonished [on their own, as just now demonstrated]?

E. Why then state, "you, or your son or your daughter"?

F. This refers to minors.

14. A. "Your manservant or your maidservant":

B. This refers to those who are within the covenant [that is, Israelites].

C. You maintain that this refers to those who are covered by the covenant. But perhaps reference is to an uncircumcised slave?

D. When Scripture says, "And the son of your slave-girl and the stranger may be refreshed" (Exod. 23:12), lo, the uncircumcised slave is covered.

E. Then why does Scripture say, "your manservant or your maidservant"?

F. This refers to those who are within the covenant [that is, Israelites].

15. A. "Nor your stranger who is within your gates":

B. This refers to the righteous proselyte.

C. Or perhaps reference is made to the resident alien?

D. When Scripture says, "And the stranger," it addresses the resident alien.

E. What then does Scripture mean by, "nor your stranger who is within your gates"?

F. This refers to the righteous proselyte.

16. A. "For in six days the Lord made heaven and earth, the sea and all that is in them":

B. This indicates that the sea weighs in the balance as equal to all the other works of creation.

17. A. "And rested on the seventh day":

B. And does fatigue affect God? Is it not said, "The creator of the ends of the earth does not faint and is not weary" (Isa. 40:28), "He gives power to the faint" (Isa. 40:29); "By the word of the Lord the heavens were made" (Ps. 33:6)?

C. How then can Scripture say, "and rested on the seventh day"?

D. It is as if [God] had it written concerning himself that he created the world in six days and rested on the seventh.

E. Now you may reason a fortiori:

F. Now if the One who is not affected by fatigue had it written concerning himself that he created the world in six days and rested on the seventh, how much the more so should a human being, concerning whom it is written, "but man is born to trouble" (Job 5:7) [also rest on the Sabbath]?

18. A. "Therefore the Lord blessed the sabbath day and hallowed it":

B. "He blessed it with manna and he hallowed it with manna," the words of R. Ishmael.

C. R. Aqiba says, "He blessed it with manna, but he hallowed it with a blessing."

D. R. Isaac says, "He blessed it with manna, but he hallowed it with the example of the man gathering wood [who was put to death for working on the Sabbath and this accomplished the perpetual sanctification of the Sabbath]."

E. R. Simeon b. Yohai says, "He blessed it with manna and hallowed it with lights."

F. R. Simeon b. Judah of Kefar Akko says in the name of R. Simeon, "He blessed it with manna and hallowed it with the light of a person's face on that day.

G. "Therefore it is said, 'therefore the Lord blessed the sabbath day and hallowed it.'"

Nos. 1–5 construct a set of examples of the same fact, that where we have duplications or contradictions, these are harmonized; God made statements that seem to contradict one another at one and the same time, indicating that there is a harmony to be discovered. Nos. 6–10 form a thematic aggregate. Nos. 11 and 12 go over the same ground, and nos. 13–15 form yet another patterned set. The net effect throughout is that the compilers have a theme, but no sharply etched proposition that they wish to demonstrate concerning that theme. The compilation succeeds in saying many valuable things about the Sabbath, but does not seem to me to make any striking and fresh points that reshape discourse overall.

That is why I characterize the document as a whole in the way I have: a scriptural encyclopaedia.

Because our authorship presents not a special viewpoint or a distinctive program of argument but a set of routine affirmations, its writing forms precisely what that authorship intended: an encyclopaedia of information, inclusive of explanation of important verses of Scripture, organized around parts of the book of Exodus. The rhetoric, the logic of cogent discourse, and the topical and propositional traits of the document all together serve precisely that simple purpose. If someone proposes to set forth a set of banalities and commonplaces, acceptable to a broad constituency as self-evidently valid propositions of the Torah, that is, to write a scriptural encyclopaedia of Judaism, Mekhilta's very inchoate propositional program, its ordinary and routine statements, its banality and conventionality of proposition—these show us how to do it.

Can we say the same of Sifra, to take one test case? I think not. The capacious rubrics just now set forth, which in theory may well serve diverse Midrash-compilations, each with its own distinctive viewpoint and intellectual method, tell us little about the topical program of Sifra in particular. True, were we to employ them in organizing the episodic sayings and opinions found in Sifra, we should find a mass of materials pertinent to a theme. But these materials do not emerge as cogent with one another in any interesting way. The three categories for Sifra constitute merely the intellectual counterpart to the logic of fixed association. For knowing the three potential categories of topics, we cannot predict the actual program of Sifra—or of any document in the canon of the Judaism of the dual Torah other than Mekhilta Attributed to R. Ishmael. Sifra does not follow any sort of topical program independent of that of the book of Leviticus, and Sifra's authorship does not set forth any propositions particular to the themes or subject matter of the book of Leviticus. But the contrary is the case for Mekhilta Attributed to R. Ishmael, as we have seen. At each point at which we found a proposition well argued, the distinctive statement of the verse of Scripture under discussion defined the topic and dictated the shaping of the proposition—for example, the salvation at the Sea: on account of what merit? By contrast, in Sifra, where discourse moves beyond Scripture, it is not toward fresh theological or philosophical thought, such as we note in Mekhilta Attributed to R. Ishmael, not to mention the Rabbah-compilations and Sifré to Deuteronomy. But each of those compilations—Genesis Rabbah, Leviticus Rabbah, Pesiqta deRab Kahana, and Sifré to Deuteronomy—makes its well-argued points also. In the case of none of them do we have so random and routine a collection of theological truths as we find assembled in our document.

It is in this context that I lay down a simple judgment. By contrast to Sifra, Mekhilta Attributed to R. Ishmael forms a statement of a principal component of "Judaism in general," that is, collects and sets forth the Judaism of the dual Torah, so far as that Judaism draws upon and amplifies the parts of the written Torah subject to discussion here. And, by contrast to Mekhilta Attributed to R. Ishmael, other Midrash-compilations do *not* exhibit that same quality of sheer banality, not at all. Each makes its own point, in its own way, for its own purpose, in response to its own ineluctable question providing its own self-evidently valid answer. The other documents make different points in answering different questions so that in plan and in program they yield more contrasts than comparisons.

PART TWO

Prophecy and the Context of Scripture

THE CLARIFICATION OF SCRIPTURE
IN THE LIGHT OF THE FUTURE

7
Prologue

SEEING THE PAST AS FUTURE HISTORY

The first stage in the formation of Midrash-compilations for Judaism shows us how to read Scripture to clarify basic questions. But how about turning to Scripture to solve problems? One model for reading Scripture as God's letter to us this morning, for today in particular, derives from the Midrash-compilations that were worked out in response to a vast historical crisis for Judaism. It is the crisis precipitated by Constantine's legalization of Christianity at the beginning of the fourth century, and the Roman Empire's selection of Christianity as official and favored religion of the state by the end of that same time. For the first time since Sinai, as "our sages of blessed memory" saw matters, the Torah as they read it faced competition with another reading of that same revelation. And what made that fact critical were the auspices under which the competing Torah, now the Bible comprising Old and New Testaments, was to be read. How to solve a problem of such dimensions?

The answer did not lay in merely collecting and reiterating information, or in merely showing connections between contemporary and ancient media of revelation, such as Mekhilta's and Sifra's authorships accomplished. Nor was it sufficient to amplify and paraphrase and generalize, as the two Sifrés' authorships did. The very bland character of the Midrash-compilations of the first type—paraphrase—attests to the serviceability of those documents to the task of speaking to the community seen as autonomous of the world. But the world out there intervened and precipitated a crisis, and on that account a new kind of Midrash-compilation had to be attempted. It was one that read Scripture not for paraphrase but for prophecy, and to that type of Midrash-compilation and the context that precipitated it we now turn.

Prophecy, of course, is a mode of theology formed in response to history, whether past or future. The great prophet said what things mean, interpreted events as they took place. Out of this deep knowledge of the meaning of events, prophets also addressed the future, certain in their knowledge of what would happen—what must happen—on account of how things were and where they clearly were heading. In its prophetic mode, Midrash-exegesis turned matters around by explaining the present out of the resources of eternity. Scripture's account of the past instructed our sages on how to explain what was happening then and told them, also, what would happen in time to come. The question of events' meaning, then, was rephrased in terms of the Scripture paradigm. Scripture, the written Torah, defined what an event was and also indicated what happening did not fall into the category of an event at all. For our sages, what that meant was simple. If you want to know what happenings really matter, fall into the category of events, you open Scripture. And what you find there is the paradigm that instructs you on what, in your own day, matters, and what does not: events, not mere happenings. From that knowledge flows the power of prophecy as Midrash-exegesis accomplishes prophecy: the capacity to interpret events by appeal to the past understood as future. That explains why Midrash-exegesis, yielding Midrash-compilations, in search of prophecy now focused upon history, meaning, the representation of intelligible sequences of purposeful events presented as narrative.

This address to Scripture as future history had no precedent in the Judaism of the dual Torah. The Judaism that had been taking shape, beginning two centuries before the Mishnah in 200, did not encompass in its canonical writings a single historical work. The writings it did produce, moreover, rarely contained much narrative or even biography of a sustained order. To define the terms of the crisis that defined the task of Midrash as prophecy is simple. Christians saw Israel as God's people, rejected by God for rejecting the Christ. Israel saw Christians, now embodied in Rome, as Ishmael, Esau, Edom: the brother and the enemy. The political revolution marked by Constantine's conversion not only forced the two parties to discuss a single agendum and defined the terms in which each would take up that agendum. It also made each party investigate the entire past in making sense of the unprecedented and uncertain present. When emperors convert and governments shift allegiance, the world shakes underfoot.

In writings prior to those brought to closure at the end of the tumultuous fourth century, sages had in general treated scriptural history as typology or, as we say, they simply amplified narratives without yielding pointed contemporaneous conclusions. No pattern of history emerged in Midrash as paraphrase so as to impose articulated meaning on contemporary events. Rather than seeing historical events as patterned and therefore producing one-time and unique, yielding lessons on their own, the authorship of the Mishnah and associated writings such as the Tosefta, Sifra, and the two Sifrés classified events in accord with the shared taxonomic traits among them. So history as a sequence of unique, linear events, coming from somewhere and going to some other goal, played no articulated role in the writing at all. The authorship of the Mishnah for its part identified regularities in discrete events, seeking the laws of the social order. They produced the opposite of history: not unique, linear happenings but patterns that applied in any age.

To appreciate the importance of the shift represented by Midrash-compilations that focused upon history and prophecy, we do well to notice how small a role history as such played in prior writings. The framers of the Mishnah, for their part, explicitly refer to very few events, treating those they do mention with a focus quite separate from the unfolding events themselves. They rarely create narratives; historical events do not supply organizing categories or taxonomic classifications. We find no tractate devoted to the destruction of the Temple, no complete chapter detailing the events of Bar Kokhba, nor even a sustained celebration of the events of the sages' own historical lives. When things that have happened are mentioned, it is neither to narrate nor to interpret and draw lessons from the events. It is either to illustrate a point of law or to pose a problem of the law—always en passant, never in a pointed way. Narrative, in the Mishnah's limited rhetorical repertoire, is reserved for the narrow framework of what priests and others do on recurrent occasions and around the Temple. In all, that staple of history, stories about dramatic events and important deeds, provides little nourishment in the minds of the Mishnah's jurisprudents. Events, if they appear at all, are treated as trivial. They may be well known, but are consequential in some way other than is revealed in the detailed account of what actually happened. Events are there to be classified.

To this labor of taxonomy, the historian's way of selecting data and arranging them into patterns of meaning to teach lessons proves inconsequential. For history writing, by contrast, what is important is to describe what is unique and individual, not what is ongoing and unremarkable. History is the story of change, development, movement, not of what does not change, develop, or move. For the thinkers of the Mishnah, on the other hand, historical patterning emerges through taxonomy, the classification of the unique and individual, the organization of change and movement within unchanging categories. In the Mishnah's system one-time events are not important. The world is composed of nature and supernature. The laws that count are those to be discovered in heaven and, in heaven's creation and counterpart, on earth. Keep those laws and things will work out. Break them, and the result is predictable: calamity of whatever sort will supervene in accordance with the rules. But just because it is predictable, a catastrophic happening testifies to what has always been and must always be, in accordance with reliable rules and within categories already discovered and well explained. That is why the lawyer-philosophers of the mid-second century produced the Mishnah —to explain how things are.

The events of the fourth century directed attention to trends and patterns, just as the framers of the Mishnah would have wanted. But in search of those trends, the detailed record of history—so far as that record made trends visible and exposed the laws of social history— demanded close study. That is why sages' response to the historical crisis of the fourth century required them to reread the records of history, as much as Eusebius resifted the facts of the past. The sedulous indifference to concrete events, except for taxonomic purposes, characteristic of the Mishnaic authorship provided no useful model. Concrete, immediate, and singular events now made a difference.

Genesis Rabbah, a work that came to closure sometime after 400, marks the beginning of Midrash as prophecy. Its authors not only lived through that period of radical political change, but also reconsidered the historical question by reverting to the record of creation, the beginnings of Israel in particular. They asked in the tradition of prophecy, What patterns do we discern to tell us where events are leading? And they found the answer in Scripture. That is why they read Scripture as this morning's newspaper, as a letter from God written in particular to them and their own circumstance.

In Leviticus Rabbah, brought to closure about fifty years later, in ca. 450, sages read Scripture in search of the rules of regularity and order that pertained, in particular, to the social order. For, like the prophets of old, they took for granted that the condition of society determined the fate of Israel, the holy people. In Pesiqta deRab Kahana, following upon and borrowing from Leviticus Rabbah, yet another authorship looked deep within the life of Israel under the aspect of eternity in quest of meaning of events in its own time.

8
Genesis Rabbah

THE RULES OF HISTORY
SET FORTH BY REVELATION

The framers of Genesis Rabbah intended to find those principles of society and of history that would permit them to make sense of the on-going history of Israel. These principles they found in Scripture, and that is how the sages formed Midrash as prophecy. They took for granted that Scripture speaks to the life and condition of Israel, the Jewish people. And that address, they understood as fact, was not to Israel in olden times alone or mainly, but to Israel in the here and now: once more, this morning's newspaper, as God would publish it in heaven!

In view of the framers of Midrash as prophecy, the entire narrative of Genesis is so formed as to point toward the sacred history of Israel, the Jewish people: its slavery and redemption; its coming Temple in Jerusalem; its exile and salvation at the end of time. In the reading of the authors at hand, therefore, the powerful message of Genesis proclaims that the world's creation commenced a single, straight line of events, leading in the end to the salvation of Israel and through Israel all humanity. That message—that history heads toward Israel's salvation—sages derived from the book of Genesis and contributed to their own day. Therefore in their reading of Scripture a given story will bear a deeper truth about what it means to be Israel, on the one side, and what in the end of days will happen to Israel, on the other. True, their reading makes no explicit reference to what, if anything, had changed in the age of Constantine. But we do find repeated references to the four kingdoms, Babylonia, Media, Greece, Rome—and beyond the fourth will come Israel, fifth and last. So sages' message, in their theology of history, was that the present anguish prefigured the coming vindication of God's people.

It follows that sages read Genesis as the history of the world with emphasis on Israel. So the lives portrayed, the domestic quarrels and petty conflicts with the neighbors, all serve to yield insight into what was to be. Why so? Because the deeds of the patriarchs taught lessons on how the children were to act, and, it further followed, the lives of the patriarchs signaled the history of Israel. Israel constituted one extended family, and the metaphor of the family, serving the nation as it did, imparted to the stories of Genesis the character of a family record. History become genealogy conveyed the message of salvation. These propositions really laid down the same judgment, one for the individual and the family, the other for the community and the nation, since there was no differentiating. Every detail of the narrative therefore served to prefigure what was to be, and Israel found itself, time and again, in the revealed facts of the history of the creation of the world, the decline of humanity down to the time of Noah, and, finally, its ascent to Abraham, Isaac, and Israel.

In Genesis Rabbah the entire narrative of Genesis is so formed as to point toward the sacred history of Israel, the Jewish people: its slavery and redemption; its coming Temple in Jerusalem; its exile and salvation at the end of time. The powerful prophetic message of Genesis in the rereading of the authorship of Genesis Rabbah proclaims that the world's creation commenced a single, straight line of significant events, that is to say, a history, leading in the end to the salvation of Israel and through Israel all humanity. If, therefore, I had to point to the single most important proposition of Genesis Rabbah, it is that, in the story of the beginnings of creation, humanity, and Israel, we find the message of the meaning and end of the life of the Jewish people. The deeds of the founders supply signals for the children about what is going to come in the future. So the biography of Abraham, Isaac, and Jacob also constitutes a protracted account of the history of Israel later on. If the sages of Judaism could announce a single syllogism and argue it systematically, that is the proposition upon which they would insist.

We may now generalize on the theory of history in Genesis Rabbah. The sages who produced that book understood that stories about the progenitors, presented in the book of Genesis, define the human condition and proper conduct for their children, Israel in time to come. Accordingly, they systematically asked Scripture to tell them how they were supposed to conduct themselves at the critical turnings of life. The first thing to notice is how a variety of events is made to prove a syllogism. The stories of Genesis therefore join stories of other times and persons in Israel's history. All of them equally, and timelessly, point to prevailing rules. Syllogistic argument, resting on lists of facts of the same classification, wrests the narrative out of its one-time and time-bound setting and turns it into a statement of rules that prevail everywhere and all the time for Israel. Here is a good example of the mode of argument of the document.

Genesis Rabbah 96

VCVI:III

1. A. "And when the time drew near that Israel must die [he called his son Joseph and said to him, 'If now I have found favor in your sight, put your hand under my thigh and promise to deal loyally and truly with me. Do not bury me in Egypt, but let me lie with my fathers; carry me out of Egypt and bury me in their burying place.' He answered, 'I will do as you have said.' And he said, 'Swear to me.' And he swore to him. Then Israel bowed himself upon the head of his bed]" (Gen. 47:29–31):

   B. "There is no man that has power of the spirit . . . neither is there dominion in the day of death" (Qoh. 8:8).

   C. Said R. Joshua of Sikhnin in the name of R. Levi, "As to the trumpets that Moses made in the wilderness, when Moses lay on the point of death, the Holy One, blessed be he, hid them away, so that he would not blow on them and summon the people to him.

   D. "This was meant to fulfill this verse: '. . . neither is there dominion in the day of death' (Qoh. 8:8).

   E. "When Zimri did his deed, what is written? 'And Phineas went after the man of Israel into the chamber' (Num. 25:8). So where was Moses, that Phineas should speak before he did?

   F. "'. . . neither is there dominion in the day of death' (Qoh. 8:8).

   G. "But the formulation expresses humiliation. Salvation was handed over to Phineas, [and Moses] abased himself.

   H. "So too with David: 'Now King David was old' (1 Kings 1:1). What is stated about him when he lay dying? 'Now the days of David drew near, that he should die' (1 Kings 2:1).

   I. "What is said is not '*king* David,' but merely 'David.'

   J. "The same applies to Jacob, when he was on the point of death, he humbled himself to Joseph, saying to him, 'If now I have found favor in your sight.' [So he abased himself, since there is no dominion on the day of death.]

   K. "When did this take place? As he drew near the end: 'And when the time drew near that Israel must die.'"

What strikes the exegete is the unprepossessing language used by Jacob in speaking to Joseph. The intersecting verse makes clear that, on the day of one's death, one no longer rules. Several examples of that fact are given, Moses, David, finally Jacob. So the syllogism about the loss of power on the occasion of death derives proof from a number of sources, and the passage has not been worked out to provide the exegesis of our base verse in particular. The exposition is all the more moving because the exegete focuses upon his proposition, rather than on the great personalities at hand. His message obviously is that even the greatest lose all dominion when they are going to die. In this way the deeds of the founders define the rule for the descendants.

As a corollary to the view that the biography of the fathers prefigures the history of the descendants, sages maintained that the deeds of the children—the holy way of life of Israel—follow the model established by the founders long ago. So they looked in Genesis for the basis for the things they held to be God's will for Israel. And they found ample proof. Sages invariably searched the stories of Genesis for evidence of the origins not only of creation and of Israel, but also of Israel's cosmic way of life, its understanding of how, in the passage of nature and the seasons, humanity worked out its relationship with God. The holy way of life that Israel lived through the seasons of nature therefore would make its mark upon the stories of the creation of the world and the beginning of Israel.

Part of the reason sages pursued the interest at hand derived from polemic. From the first Christian century theologians of Christianity maintained that salvation did not depend upon keeping the laws of the Torah. Abraham, after all, had been justified and he did not keep the Torah, which, in his day, had not yet been given. So sages time and again would maintain that Abraham indeed kept the entire Torah even before it had been revealed. They further attributed to Abraham, Isaac, and Jacob rules of the Torah enunciated only later on, for example, the institution of prayer three times a day. But the passage before us bears a different charge. It is to Israel to see how deeply embedded in the rules of reality were the patterns governing God's relationship to Israel. That relationship, one of human sin and atonement, divine punishment and forgiveness, expresses the most fundamental laws of human existence. Here is yet another rule that tells sages what to find in Scripture.

Genesis Rabbah 98

XCVIII:I

1. A.   "Then Jacob called his sons [and said, 'Gather yourselves together, that I may tell you what shall befall you in days to come. Assemble and hear, O sons of Jacob, and hearken to Israel, your father. Reuben, you are my firstborn, my might and the first fruits of my strength, preeminent in pride and preeminent in power. Unstable as water, you shall not have preeminence, because you went up to your father's bed, then you defiled it, you went up to my couch!']" (Gen. 49:1-4):

B. "I will cry to God Most High [unto God who completes it for me]" (Ps. 57:3):

C. "I will cry to God Most High": on the New Year.

D. "... unto God who completes it for me": on the Day of Atonement.

E. To find out which [goat] is for the Lord and which one is for an evil decree.

2. A. Another matter: "I will cry to God Most High [unto God who completes it for me]" (Ps. 57:3):

B. "I will cry to God Most High": refers to our father, Jacob.

C. "... unto God who completes it for me": for the Holy One, blessed be he, concurred with him to give each of the sons a blessing in accord with his character.

D. "Then Jacob called his sons [and said, 'Gather yourselves together, that I may tell you what shall befall you in days to come].'"

The intersecting verse invites the comparison of the judgment of the Days of Awe to the blessing of Jacob, and that presents a dimension of meaning that the narrative would not otherwise reveal. Just as God decides which goat serves what purpose, so God concurs in Jacob's judgment of which son/tribe deserves what sort of blessing. So Jacob stands in the stead of God in this stunning comparison of Jacob's blessing to the day of judgment. The link between Jacob's biography and the holy life of Israel is fresh.

What, then, tells sages how to identify the important and avoid the trivial? The answer derives from the fundamental theological conviction that gives life to their search of Scripture. It is that the task of Israel is to hope, and the message of Genesis—there for the sages to uncover and make explicit—is always to hope. For a Jew it is a sin to despair. This I think defines the iron law of meaning, telling sages what matters and what does not, guiding their hands to take up those verses that permit expression of hope—that above all. Given the definitive event of their day—the conversion of the great empire of Rome to Christianity—the task of hope proved not an easy assignment.

XCVIII:XIV

3. A. "I hope for your salvation, O Lord" (Gen. 49:18):

B. Said R. Isaac, "All things depend on hope, suffering depends on hope, the sanctification of God's name depends on hope, the merit attained by the fathers depends on hope, the lust for the age to come depends on hope.

C. "That is in line with this verse: 'Yes, in the way of your judgments, O Lord, we have hoped for you, to your name, and to your memorial, is the desire of our soul' (Isa. 26:8). 'The way of your judgments refers to suffering.

D.   "'. . . to your name': this refers to the sanctification of the divine name.
E.   "'. . . and to your memorial': this refers to the merit of the fathers.
F.   "'. . . is the desire of our soul': this refers to the lust for the age to come.
G.   "Grace depends on hope: 'O Lord, be gracious to us, we have hoped for you' (Isa. 33:2).
H.   "Forgiveness depends on hope: 'For with you is forgiveness' (Ps. 133:4), then: 'I hope for the Lord'" (Ps. 130:5).

The interesting unit is no. 4, which is explicit on the critical importance of hope in the salvific process, and which further links the exclamation to the setting in which it occurs. This seems to me to typify the strength of the exegesis at hand, with its twin powers to link all details to a tight narrative and to link the narrative to the history of Israel.

Sages read the narrative of creation and the fall of Adam to testify to the redemption and the salvation of Israel. The following passage provides a stunning example of the basic theory of sages on how the stories of creation are to be read:

Genesis Rabbah 29
XXIX:III

1.   A.   "And Noah found grace" (Gen. 6:8):
     B.   Said R. Simon, "'There were three acts of finding on the part of the Holy One, blessed be he:
     C.   "'And you found [Abraham's] heart faithful before you' (Neh. 9:8).
     D.   "'I have found David my servant' (Ps. 89:21).
     E.   "'I found Israel like grapes in the wilderness'" (Hos. 9:10).
     F.   His fellows said to R. Simon, "And is it not written, 'Noah found grace in the eyes of the Lord'" (Gen. 6:8)?
     G.   He said to them, "He found it, but the Holy One, blessed be he, did not find it."
     H.   Said R. Simon, "He found grace in the wilderness' (Jer. 31:2) on account of the merit of the generation of the wilderness."

The proposition draws on the verse at hand, but makes its own point. It is that the grace shown to Noah derived from Israel. Noah on his own—that is, humanity—enjoyed salvation only because of Israel's merit. The proposition is striking and daring. God "found," that is, made an accidental discovery, of a treasure, consisting only of three: Abraham, David, and Israel. These stand for the beginning, the end, and the holy people that started with Abraham and found redemption through David. As if to underline this point, we refer H to the generation of the Wilderness and its faith, which merited gaining the land.

A cogent and uniform worldview accompanied the sages at hand when they approached the text of Genesis. This worldview they systematically joined to that text, fusing the tale at hand with that larger context of imagination in which the tale was received and read. Accordingly, when we follow the sages' mode of interpreting the text, we find our way deep into their imaginative life. Scripture becomes the set of facts that demonstrate the truth of the syllogisms that encompassed and described the world, as sages saw it. The next stage in my demonstration of the systematic and deeply polemical reading at hand will take the simple form of successive illustration of the basic thesis. That thesis is that Israel's salvific history informs and infuses the creation of the world. That story takes on its true meaning from what happened to Israel, and it follows that Israel's future history accounts for the creation of the world.

Genesis Rabbah 20

XX:I

1. A. "Then the Lord God said to the serpent, 'Because you have done this, cursed are you above all cattle and above all wild animals'" (Gen. 3:14):
   B. "A slanderer shall not be established in the earth; the violent and wicked man shall be hunted with thrust upon thrust" (Ps. 140:12).
   C. Said R. Levi, "In the world to come the Holy One, blessed be he, will take the nations of the world and bring them down to Gehenna. He will say to them, 'Why did you impose fines upon my children?' They will say to him, 'Some of them slandered others among them. The Holy One, blessed be he, will then take these [Israelite slanderers] and those and bring them down to Gehenna."
2. A. Another interpretation: "A slanderer" refers to the snake, who slandered his creator.
   B. "Will not be established [standing upright] on earth": "Upon your belly you shall go" (Gen. 3:14).
   C. "The violent and wicked man shall be hunted": What is written is not "with a thrust" but "with thrust after thrust" [since not only the serpent was cursed]. What is written is "thrust after thrust," for man was cursed, woman was cursed, and the snake was cursed.
   D. "And the Lord God said to the serpent. . . ."

We have an exegesis of a base verse and intersecting verse, which is in that "classic" form in which the intersecting verse is fully worked out and only then drawn to meet the base verse. No. 1 treats the intersecting verse as a statement on its own, and then no. 2 reads the verse in line with Gen. 3:14. But the intersecting verse is hardly chosen at random,

since it speaks of slander in general, and then at no. 2 the act of slander of
the snake is explicitly read into the intersecting verse. So the intersection
is not only thematic, not by any means. The upshot of the exercise links
Israel's history to the history of humanity in the garden of Eden. No. 1
focuses upon the sacred history of Israel, making the point that slan-
derers in Israel cause the nation's downfall, just as the snake caused the
downfall of humanity.

Genesis Rabbah 19

XIX:VII

1. A. "And they heard the sound of the Lord God walking in the garden in
       the cool of the day" (Gen. 3:8):
2. A. Said R. Abba bar Kahana, "The word is not written, 'move,' but
       rather, 'walk,' bearing the sense that [the Presence of God] leapt about
       and jumped upward.
   B. "[The point is that God's presence leapt upward from the earth on
       account of the events in the garden, as will now be explained:] The
       principal location of the Presence of God was [meant to be] among the
       creatures down here. When the first man sinned, the Presence of God
       moved up to the first firmament. When Cain sinned, it went up to the
       second firmament. When the generation of Enosh sinned, it went up
       to the third firmament. When the generation of the Flood sinned, it
       went up to the fourth firmament. When the generation of the dis-
       persion [at the tower of Babel] sinned, it went up to the fifth. On
       account of the Sodomites it went up to the sixth, and on account of the
       Egyptians in the time of Abraham it went up to the seventh.
   C. "But, as a counterpart, there were seven righteous men who rose up:
       Abraham, Isaac, Jacob, Levi, Kahath, Amram, and Moses. They
       brought the Presence of God [by stages] down to earth.
   D. "Abraham brought it from the seventh to the sixth, Isaac brought it
       from the sixth to the fifth, Jacob brought it from the fifth to the fourth,
       Levi brought it down from the fourth to the third, Kahath brought it
       down from the third to the second, Amram brought it down from the
       second to the first. Moses brought it down to earth."
   E. Said R. Isaac, "It is written, 'The righteous will inherit the land and
       dwell therein forever' (Ps. 37:29). Now what will the wicked do? Are
       they going to fly in the air? But that the wicked did not make it
       possible for the Presence of God to take up residence on earth [is what
       the verse wishes to say]."

What is striking is the claim that while the wicked (gentiles) drove
God out of the world, the righteous (Israelites) brought God back into
the world. This theme links the story of the fall of man to the history of

Israel, with Israel serving as the counterpart and fulfillment of the fall at creation. The next composition still more strikingly shows that the creation and fall of man finds its counterpart in the formation and sanctification of Israel. So Israel serves, as did the first man, as the embodiment of humanity. But while Adam sinned and was driven from paradise, Israel through atonement will bring humanity salvation. In this way the book of Genesis serves a purpose quite pertinent to the theological program of the compilers of Genesis Rabbah.

XIX:IX

1. A. "And the Lord God called to the man and said to him, 'Where are you?'" (Gen. 3:9):
    B. [The word for "where are you" yields consonants that bear the meaning] "How has this happened to you?"
    C. [God speaks:] "Yesterday it was in accord with my plan, and now it is in accord with the plan of the snake. Yesterday it was from one end of the world to the other [that you filled the earth], and now: 'Among the trees of the garden' (Gen. 3:8) [you hide out]."
2. A. R. Abbahu in the name of R. Yosé bar Haninah: "It is written, 'But they are like a man [Adam], they have transgressed the covenant' (Hos. 6:7).
    B. "'They are like a man,' specifically, like the first man. [We shall now compare the story of the first man in Eden with the story of Israel in its land.]
    C. "'In the case of the first man, I brought him into the garden of Eden, I commanded him, he violated my commandment, I judged him to be sent away and driven out, but I mourned for him, saying "How . . ."'" [which begins the book of Lamentations, hence stands for a lament, but which, as we just saw, also is written with the consonants that also yield, 'Where are you'].
    D. "'I brought him into the garden of Eden,' as it is written, 'And the Lord God took the man and put him into the garden of Eden' (Gen. 2:15).
    E. "'I commanded him,' as it is written, 'And the Lord God commanded . . .' (Gen. 2:16).
    F. "'And he violated my commandment,' as it is written, 'Did you eat from the tree concerning which I commanded you?' (Gen. 3:11).
    G. "'I judged him to be sent away,' as it is written, 'And the Lord God sent him from the garden of Eden' (Gen. 3:23).
    H. "'And I judged him to be driven out.' 'And he drove out the man' (Gen. 3:24).
    I. "'But I mourned for him, saying, "How . . .".' 'And he said to him, "Where are you?"' (Gen. 3:9), and the word for 'where are you' is written, 'How. . . .'

J.   "'So too in the case of his descendants [God continues to speak] I brought them into the Land of Israel, I commanded them, they violated my commandment, I judged them to be sent out and driven away but I mourned for them, saying,'How. . . .'"

K.   "'I brought them into the Land of Israel.' 'And I brought you into the land of Carmel' (Jer. 2:7).

L.   "'I commanded them.' 'And you, command the children of Israel' (Exod. 27:20). 'Command the children of Israel' (Lev. 24:2).

M.   "'They violated my commandment.' 'And all Israel have violated your Torah' (Dan. 9:11).

N.   "'I judged them to be sent out.' 'Send them away, out of my sight and let them go forth' (Jer. 15:1).

O.   "'. . .and driven away.' 'From my house I shall drive them' (Hos. 9:15).

P.   "But I mourned for them, saying, 'How. . . .' 'How has the city sat solitary, that was full of people'" (Lam. 1:1).

No. 1 simply contrasts one day with the next, a stunning and stark statement, lacking all decoration. No. 1 certainly sets the stage for no. 2 and the whole must be regarded as a cogent, thoughtful composition. The other, no. 2, equally simply compares the story of man in the Garden of Eden with the tale of Israel in its land. Every detail is in place, the articulation is perfect, and the result is completely convincing as an essay in interpretation. All this rests on the simple fact that the word for "where are you" may be expressed as "How . . . ," which, as is clear, invokes the opening words of the book of Lamentations. So Israel's history serves as a paradigm for human history, and vice versa. What then is the point? It is obedience, as the following indicates:

XIX:XI

1.   A.   "The man said, 'The woman whom you gave to be with me gave me fruit of the tree, and I ate'" (Gen. 3:12):

B.   There are four on whose pots the Holy One, blessed be he, knocked, only to find them filled with piss, and these are they: Adam, Cain, the wicked Balaam, and Hezekiah.

C.   Adam: "The man said, 'The woman whom you gave to be with me gave me fruit of the tree and I ate'" (Gen. 3:12).

D.   Cain: "And the Lord said to Cain, 'Where is Abel, your brother?'" (Gen. 4:9).

E.   The wicked Balaam: "And God came to Balaam and said, 'What men are these with you?'" (Num. 22:9)

F.   Hezekiah: "Then came Isaiah the prophet to king Hezekiah and said to him, 'What did these men say?'" (2 Kings. 20:14).

G.   But Ezekiel turned out to be far more adept than any of these: "'Son of

man, can these bones live?' And I said, 'O Lord God, you know'"
(Ezek. 37:3).

H. Said R., Hinena bar Pappa, "The matter may be compared to the case
of a bird that was caught by a hunter. The hunter met someone who
asked him, 'Is this bird alive or dead?'

I. "He said to him, 'If you want, it is alive, but if you prefer, it is dead.'
So: 'Will these bones live?' And he said, 'Lord God, you know.'"

The colloquy once more serves to find in Israel's history a counterpart
to the incident at hand. Only Ezekiel knew how to deal with a question
that bore with it the answer: God will do as he likes, God knows the
answer. That is, the sole appropriate response is one of humility and
acceptance of God's will. With what result? With the result of the
salvation of humanity through Israel. History through Israel becomes
the story of the salvation of humanity:

XXI:I

1. A. "Then the Lord God said, 'Behold, the man has become like one of us
    [knowing good and evil, and now, lest he put forth his hand and take
    also of the tree of life and eat and live forever]'" (Gen. 3:22):

    B. "It is written, 'Then I heard a holy one speaking, and another holy one
    said to that certain one who spoke'" (Dan. 8:13).

    C. "The one" refers to the Holy One, blessed be he: "The Lord, our God,
    the Lord is One" (Deut. 6:4).

    D. "Holy," for everyone says before him, "Holy. . . . "

    E. "Speaking" means "issuing harsh decrees against his creatures."

    F. [For example] "Thorns and thistles it shall bring forth to you" (Gen.
    3:18).

    G. "And another holy one said to that certain one who spoke":

    H. R. Huna said, "It was to Mr. So-and-So."

    I. Aqilas translated the passage, "It was to one who was within that he
    spoke, meaning the first man, whose presence lay within [and closer
    to God than] that of the serving angels [since he stood closer to God
    than they did]." [The remainder of the exegesis flows from Aqilas's
    view of the locus of discourse.]

    J. "How long shall be the vision concerning the continual burnt offer-
    ing?" (Dan. 8:13):

    K. "Will the decree that has been issued against the first man go on
    forever?"

    L. "And the transgression that causes desolation" (Deut. 8:13):

    M. "So too will his transgression desolate him even in the grave?"

    N. "To give both the sanctuary and the host to be trampled underfoot"
    (Dan. 8:13):

O.   "Will he and his descendants be made into chaff before the angel of
     death?"
P.   "And he said to me, 'Until evening, morning two thousand and three
     hundred, then shall the sanctuary be victorious'" (Dan. 8:14):
Q.   R. Azariah, R. Jonathan b. Haggai in the name of R. Isaac: "In any
     case in which it is evening, it is not morning, and in any case in which
     it is morning, it surely is not evening. [So what is the sense of this
     passage?] But when it is morning for the nations of the world, it is
     evening for Israel, and as to 'morning,' at that time [at which it is
     morning for Israel], then 'shall the sanctuary be victorious,' for at that
     time I shall declare him justified of that decree: 'Behold, let the man
     become like one of us'" (Gen. 3:22).

The fully exploited intersection of the intersecting and base verses
turns the statement of Gen. 3:22 into a powerful promise. Man will
indeed become like the One, at the time that the gentiles reach their
evening, and Israel, morning. So once more the condition of Israel serves
as a paradigm for the human situation, but this in a most concrete and
specific way. The nations of the world embody the curse of God to man,
and Israel, the promised future blessing. The framer of the passage
carefully avoids speculation on the meaning of the numbers used in
Daniel's passage, so the apocalyptic power of Daniel's vision serves the
rather generalized messianic expectations of sages, without provoking
dangerous speculation on the here and now.

XXI:VII

3.   A.   Judah b. Padaiah interpreted, "Who will remove the dust from
          between your eyes, O first man! For you could not abide in the
          commandment that applied to you for even a single hour, and lo, your
          children can wait for three years to observe the prohibition of the use
          of the fruit of a tree for the first three years after it is planted: 'Three
          years shall it be as forbidden to you, it shall not be eaten'" (Lev.
          19:23).
     B.   Said R. Huna, "When Bar Qappara heard this, he said, 'Well have you
          expounded matters, Judah, son of my sister!'"

No. 3 then compares the character of Israel to the character of the first
man, calling Israel "descendants of the first man" and pointing out that
they can observe a commandment for a long time. The example is apt,
since Israel observes the prohibition involving the fruit of a newly
planted tree, and does so for three years, while the first man could not
keep his hands off a fruit tree for even an hour. This of course restates
with enormous power the fact that Israel's history forms the counterpart
to the history of humanity. But while the first man could not do what

God demanded, Israel can and does do God's will. We come at the end to a simple and clear statement of the main point of it all:

Genesis Rabbah 83

LXXXIII:V

1.   A.   Wheat, straw, and stubble had a fight.
     B.   Wheat said, "It was on my account that the field was sown."
     C.   Stubble said, "It was on my account that the field was sown."
     D.   Wheat said, "The day will come and you will see."
     E.   When the harvest time came, the householder began to take the stubble and burn it, and the straw and spread it, but the wheat he made into heaps.
     F.   Everyone began to kiss the wheat. [I assume this is a reference to the messianic passage "Kiss the son," which is also to be translated, "Kiss the wheat" (Ps. 2:12).]
     G.   So too Israel and the nations of the world have a fight.
     H.   These say, "It was on our account that the world was created," and those say, "It was on our account that the world was created."
     I.   Israel says, "The day will come and you will see."
     J.   In the age to come: "You shall fan them and the wind will carry them away" (Isa. 41:16).
     K.   As to Israel: "And you shall rejoice in the Lord, you shall glory in the Holy One of Israel" (Isa. 41:16).

Here at the end sages make explicit their basic view. The world was created for Israel, and not for the nations of the world. At the end of days everyone will see what only Israel now knows. Because sages read Genesis as the history of the world with emphasis on Israel, the lives portrayed, the domestic quarrels and petty conflicts with the neighbors, as much as the story of creation itself, all serve to yield insight into what was to be. We now turn to a detailed examination of how sages spelled out the historical law at hand. The lives of the patriarchs signaled the history of Israel. Every detail of the narrative therefore served to prefigure what was to be, and Israel found itself, time and again, in the revealed facts of the history of the creation of the world, the decline of humanity down to the time of Noah, and, finally, its ascent to Abraham, Isaac, and Israel. In order to illustrate the single approach to diverse stories, whether concerning creation, Adam, and Noah, or concerning Abraham, Isaac, and Jacob, we focus on two matters, Abraham, on the one side, and Rome, on the other. In the former we see that Abraham serves as well as Adam to prove the point of it all. In the latter we observe how, in reading Genesis, the sages who compiled Genesis Rabbah discovered the meaning of the events of their own day.

A matter of deep concern focused sages' attention on the sequence of world empires to which, among other nations, Israel was subjugated, Babylonia, Media, Greece, and Rome—Rome above all. What will follow? Sages maintained that beyond the rule of Rome lay the salvation of Israel:

Genesis Rabbah 42

XLII:IV

1. A. "And it came to pass in the days of Amraphel" (Gen. 14:1):
4. A. Another matter: "And it came to pass in the days of Amraphel, king of Shinar" (Gen. 14:1) refers to Babylonia.
   B. "Arioch, king of Ellasar" (Gen. 14:1) refers to Greece.
   C. "Chedorlaomer, king of Elam" (Gen. 14:1) refers to Media.
   D. "And Tidal, king of Goiim [nations]" (Gen. 14:1) refers to the wicked government [Rome], which conscripts troops from all the nations of the world.
   E. Said R. Eleazar bar Abina, "If you see that the nations contend with one another, look for the footsteps of the king-messiah. You may know that that is the case, for lo, in the time of Abraham, because the kings struggled with one another, a position of greatness came to Abraham."

Obviously, no. 4 presents the most important reading of Gen. 14:1, for it links the events of the life of Abraham to the history of Israel and even ties the whole to the messianic expectation. I suppose that any list of four kings will provoke inquiry into the relationship of the entries of that list to the four kingdoms among which history, in Israel's experience, is divided. The process of history flows in both directions. Just as what Abraham did prefigured the future history of Israel, so what the Israelites later on were to do imposed limitations on Abraham. Time and again events in the lives of the patriarchs prefigure the four monarchies, among which, of course, the fourth, last, and most intolerable was Rome. Here is another such exercise in the recurrent proof of a single proposition.

Genesis Rabbah 44

XLIV:XVII

4. A. "[And it came to pass, as the sun was going down] lo, a deep sleep fell on Abram, and lo, a dread and great darkness fell upon him" (Gen. 15:12):
   B. ". . . lo, a dread" refers to Babylonia, as it is written, "Then was Nebuchadnezzar filled with fury" (Gen. 3:19).

C.   "and darkness" refers to Media, which darkened the eyes of Israel by making it necessary for the Israelites to fast and conduct public mourning.

D.   ". . . great . . ." refers to Greece.

E.   R. Simon said, "The kingdom of Greece set up one hundred and twenty commanders, one hundred and twenty hyparchs, and one hundred and twenty generals."

F.   Rabbis said, "It was sixty of each, as it is written, 'Serpents, fiery serpents, and scorpions' (Gen. 8:15). Just as the scorpion produces sixty eggs at a time, so the kingdom of Greece set up sixty at a time."

G.   ". . . fell upon him" refers to Edom, as it is written, "The earth quakes at the noise of their fall" (Jer. 49:21).

H.   Some reverse matters:

I.   ". . . fell upon him" refers to Babylonia, since it is written, "Fallen, fallen is Babylonia" (Isa. 21:9).

J.   ". . . great . . ." refers to Media, in line with this verse: "King Ahasuerus did make great" (Esther 3:1).

K.   "and darkness" refers to Greece, which darkened the eyes of Israel by its harsh decrees.

L.   ". . . lo, a dread" refers to Edom, as it is written, "After this I saw . . . a fourth beast, dreadful and terrible" (Dan. 7:7).

No. 4 successfully links the cited passage once more to the history of Israel. Israel's history falls under God's dominion. Whatever will happen carries out God's plan. The fourth kingdom is part of that plan, which we can discover by carefully studying Abraham's life and God's word to him. What of Rome in particular? Edom, Ishmael, and Esau all stand for Rome, perceived as a special problem, an enemy who also is a brother. In calling now-Christian Rome brother, sages conceded the Christian claim to share in the patrimony of Israel. For example, Ishmael, standing for Christian Rome, claims God's blessing, but Isaac gets it, as Jacob will take it from Esau.

Genesis Rabbah 47

XLVII:V

1.   A.   "God said, 'No, but Sarah your wife [shall bear you a son, and you shall call his name Isaac. I will establish my covenant with him as an everlasting covenant for his descendants after him]. As for Ishmael, I have heard you. Behold, I will bless him and make him fruitful and multiply him exceedingly. He shall be the father of twelve princes, and I will make him a great nation'" (Gen. 17:19–20).

     B.   R. Yohanan in the name of R. Joshua b. Hananiah, "In this case the son of the servant-woman might learn from what was said concerning the son of the mistress of the household:

    C.   "'Behold, I will bless him' refers to Isaac.

    D.   "'. . . and make him fruitful' refers to Isaac.

    E.   "'. . . and multiply him exceedingly' refers to Isaac.

    F.   "'. . . As for Ishmael, I have informed you' through the angel." [The point is, Freedman, *Genesis Rabbah* (London, 1948), p. 401, n. 4, explains, Ishmael could be sure that his blessing too would be fulfilled.]

    G.   R. Abba bar Kahana in the name of R. Birai: "Here the son of the mistress of the household might learn from the son of the handmaiden:

    H.   "'Behold, I will bless him' refers to Ishmael.

    I.   "'. . . and make him fruitful' refers to Ishmael.

    J.   "'. . . and multiply him exceedingly' refers to Ishmael.

    K.   "And by an argument a fortiori: 'But I will establish my covenant with Isaac'" (Gen. 17:21).

2. A.   Said R. Isaac, "It is written, 'All these are the twelve tribes of Israel' (Gen. 49:28). These were the descendants of the mistress [Sarah].

    B.   "But did Ishmael not establish twelve?

    C.   "The reference to those twelve is to princes, in line with the following verse: 'As princes and wind' (Prov. 25:14). [But the word for *prince* also stands for the word *vapor*, and hence the glory of the sons of Ishmael would be transient (Freedman, p. 402, n. 2).]

    D.   "But as to these tribes [descended from Isaac], they are in line with this verse: 'Sworn are the tribes of the word, selah'" (Hab. 3:9). [Freedman, p. 402, n. 3: The word for *tribe* and for *staff* or *rod*, in the cited verse, are synonyms, both meaning tribes, both meaning rods, and so these tribes would endure like rods that are planted.]

Nos. 1 and 2 take up the problem of the rather fulsome blessing assigned to Ishmael. One authority reads the blessing to refer to Isaac, the other maintains that the blessing refers indeed to Ishmael, and Isaac will gain that much more. No. 2 goes over the same issue, now with the insistence that the glory of Ishmael will pass like vapor, while the tribes of Isaac will endure as well-planted rods. The polemic against Edom/Rome, with its transient glory, is familiar.

Why Rome in the form it takes in Genesis Rabbah? And why the obsessive character of sages' disposition of the theme of Rome? Were their picture merely of Rome as tyrant and destroyer of the Temple, we should have no reason to link the text to the problems of the age of redaction and closure. But now it is Rome as Israel's brother, counterpart, and nemesis, Rome as the one thing standing in the way of Israel's, and the world's, ultimate salvation. So the stakes are different, and much higher. It is not a political Rome but a Christian and messianic Rome that is at issue: Rome as surrogate for Israel, Rome as obstacle to Israel.

Why? It is because Rome now confronts Israel with a crisis, and, I argue, the program of Genesis Rabbah constitutes a response to that crisis. Rome in the fourth century became Christian. Sages respond by facing that fact quite squarely and saying, "Indeed, it is as you say, a kind of Israel, an heir of Abraham as your texts explicitly claim. But we remain the sole legitimate Israel, the bearer of the birthright—we and not you. So you are our brother: Esau, Ishmael, Edom." And the rest follows.

By rereading the story of the beginnings, sages discovered the answer and the secret of the end. Rome claimed to be Israel, and, indeed, sages conceded, Rome shared the patrimony of Israel. That claim took the form of the Christian appropriation of the Torah as "the Old Testament," so sages acknowledged a simple fact in acceding to the notion that, in some way, Rome too formed part of Israel. But it was the rejected part, the Ishmael, the Esau, not the Isaac, not the Jacob. The advent of Christian Rome precipitated the sustained, polemical, and, I think, rigorous and well-argued rereading of beginnings in light of the end. Rome then marked the conclusion of human history as Israel had known it. Beyond? The coming of the true Messiah, the redemption of Israel, the salvation of the world, the end of time. So the issues were not inconsiderable, and when the sages spoke of Esau/Rome, as they did so often, they confronted the life-or-death decision of the day.

Let us see a simple example of how ubiquitous is the shadow of Ishmael/Esau/Edom/Rome. Whenever sages reflect on future history, their minds turn to their own day. They found the hour difficult, because Rome, now Christian, claimed that very birthright and blessing that they understood to be theirs alone. Christian Rome posed a threat without precedent. Now another dominion, besides Israel's, claimed the rights and blessings that sustained Israel. Wherever in Scripture they turned, sages found comfort in the iteration that the birthright, the blessing, the Torah, and the hope—all belonged to them and to none other. As the several antagonists of Israel stand for Rome in particular, so the traits of Rome, as sages perceived them, characterized the biblical heroes. Esau provided a favorite target. From the womb Israel and Rome contended.

Genesis Rabbah 63

LXIII:VI

1. A. "And the children struggled together [within her, and she said, 'If it is thus, why do I live?' So she went to inquire of the Lord. And the Lord said to her, 'Two nations are in your womb, and two peoples, born of you, shall be divided; the one shall be stronger than the other, and the elder shall serve the younger'] " (Gen. 25:22–23):

B.   R. Yohanan and R. Simeon b. Laqish:

C.   R. Yohanan said, "[Because the word 'struggle' contains the letters for the word 'run'] this one was running to kill that one and that one was running to kill this one."

D.   R. Simeon b. Laqish: "This one releases the laws given by that one, and that one releases the laws given by this one."

2. A.   R. Berekhiah in the name of R. Levi said, "It is so that you should not say that it was only after he left his mother's womb that [Esau] contended against [Jacob].

B.   "But even while he was yet in his mother's womb, his fist was stretched forth against him: 'The wicked stretch out their fists [so Freedman] from the womb'" (Ps. 58:4).

3. A.   "And the children struggled together within her":

B.   [Once more referring to the letters of the word "struggled," with special attention to the ones that mean "run"] they wanted to run within her.

C.   When she went by houses of idolatry, Esau would kick, trying to get out: "The wicked are estranged from the womb" (Ps. 58:4).

D.   When she went by synagogues and study houses, Jacob would kick, trying to get out: "Before I formed you in the womb, I knew you" (Jer. 1:5).

Nos. 1–3 take for granted that Esau represents Rome, and Jacob, Israel. Consequently the verse underlines the point that there is natural enmity between Israel and Rome. Esau hated Israel even while he was still in the womb. Jacob, for his part, revealed from the womb those virtues that would characterize him later on, eager to serve God as Esau was eager to worship idols

LXIII:VII

2. A.   "Two nations are in your womb [and two peoples, born of you, shall be divided; the one shall be stronger than the other, and the elder shall serve the younger]" (Gen. 25:23):

B.   There are two proud nations in your womb, this one takes pride in his world, and that one takes pride in his world.

C.   This one takes pride in his monarchy, and that one takes pride in his monarchy.

D.   There are two proud nations in your womb.

E.   Hadrian represents the nations, Solomon, Israel.

F.   There are two who are hated by the nations in your womb. All the nations hate Esau, and all the nations hate Israel.

G.   [Following Freedman's reading:] The one whom your creator hates is in your womb: "And Esau I hated" (Mal. 1:3).

The syllogism invokes the base verse as part of its repertoire of cases. No. 2 augments the statement at hand, still more closely linking it to the history of Israel. What follows explicitly introduces the issue of the Messiah:

LXIII:VIII

3. A. "The first came forth red:"
   B. R. Haggai in the name of R. Isaac: "On account of the merit attained by obeying the commandment, 'You will take for yourself on the first day . . . ' (Lev. 23:40),
   C. "I shall reveal myself to you as the First, avenge you on the first, rebuild the first, and bring you the first.
   D. "I shall reveal myself to you the First: 'I am the first and I am the last' (Isa. 44:6).
   E. ". . . avenge you on the first: 'Esau, the first came forth red.'
   F. ". . . rebuild the first: that is the Temple, of which it is written, 'You throne of glory, on high from the first, you place of our sanctuary' (Jer. 17:12).
   G. ". . . and bring you the first: that is, the messiah-king: 'A first unto Zion will I give, behold, behold them, and to Jerusalem'" (Isa. 41:27).

LXIII:X

1. A. "[When the boys grew up] Esau was a skilful hunter [a man of the field, while Jacob was a quiet man, dwelling in tents]" (Gen. 25:27):
   B. He hunted people through snaring them in words [as the Roman prosecutors do:] "Well enough, you did not steal. But who stole with you? You did not kill, but who killed with you?"
2. A. R. Abbahu said, "He was a trapper and a fieldsman, trapping at home and in the field.
   B. "He trapped at home: 'How do you tithe salt?' [which does not, in fact, have to be tithed at all!]
   C. "He trapped in the field: 'How do people give tithe for straw?' [which does not, in fact, have to be tithed at all!]"
3. A. R. Hiyya bar Abba said, "He treated himself as totally without responsibility for himself, like a field [on which anyone tramples].
   B. "Said the Israelites before the Holy One, blessed be he, 'Lord of all ages, is it not enough for us that you have subjugated us to the seventy nations, but even to this one, who is subjected to sexual intercourse just like a woman?'
   C. "Said to them the Holy One, blessed be he, 'I too will exact punishment from him with those same words: And the heart of the mighty men of Edom at that day shall be as the heart of a woman in her pangs'" (Jer. 49:22).

4. A.   "... while Jacob was a quiet man, dwelling in tents" (Gen. 25:27):
    B.   There is a reference to two tents, that is, the school house of Shem
         and the school house of Eber.

Nos. 1–3 deal with the description of Esau, explaining why he was
warlike and aggressive. Nothing Esau did proved sincere. He was a
hypocrite, even when he tried to please his parents.

Genesis Rabbah 65

LXV:I

1. A.   "When Esau was forty years old, he took to wife Judith, the daughter
         of Beeri, the Hittite, and Basemath the daughter of Elon the Hittite;
         and they made life bitter for Isaac and Rebecca" (Gen. 26:34–35):
    B.   "The swine out of the wood ravages it, that which moves in the field
         feeds on it" (Ps. 80:14).
    C.   R. Phineas and R. Hilqiah in the name of R. Simon: "Among all of the
         prophets, only two of them spelled out in public [the true character of
         Rome, represented by the swine], Asaf and Moses.
    D.   "Asaf: 'The swine out of the wood ravages it.'
    E.   "Moses: 'And the swine, because he parts the hoof' (Deut. 14:8).
    F.   "Why does Moses compare Rome to the swine? Just as the swine,
         when it crouches, puts forth its hoofs as if to say, 'I am clean,' so the
         wicked kingdom steals and grabs, while pretending to be setting up
         courts of justice.
    G.   "So Esau, for all forty years, hunted married women, ravished them,
         and when he reached the age of forty, he presented himself to his
         father, saying, 'Just as father got married at the age of forty, so I shall
         marry a wife at the age of forty.'
    H.   "When Esau was forty years old, he took to wife Judith, the daughter
         of Beeri, the Hittite, and Basemath the daughter of Elon the Hittite."

The exegesis of course once more identifies Esau with Rome. The
roundabout route linking the fact at hand, Esau's taking a wife, passes
through the territory of Roman duplicity. Whatever the government
does, it claims to do in the general interest. But it really has no public
interest at all. Esau for his part spent forty years pillaging women and
then, at the age of forty, pretended, to his father, to be upright. That, at
any rate, is the parallel clearly intended by this obviously unitary composition. The issue of the selection of the intersecting verse does not
present an obvious solution to me; it seems to me only the identification
of Rome with the swine accounts for the choice. The contrast between
Israel and Esau produced the following anguished observation. But here
the Rome is not yet Christian, so far as the clear reference is concerned.

The union of the two principal motifs of exegesis, the paradigmatic character of the lives of the patriarchs and matriarchs, the messianic message derived from those lives, is effected in the following:

Genesis Rabbah 83

LXXXIII:I

1. A. "These are the kings who reigned in the land of Edom before any king reigned over the Israelites: Bela the son of Beor reigned in Edom, the name of his city being Dinhabah" (Gen. 36:31–32):
    B. R. Isaac commenced discourse by citing this verse: "Of the oaks of Bashan they have made your oars" (Ezek. 27:6).
    C. Said R. Isaac, "The nations of the world are to be compared to a ship. Just as a ship has its mast made in one place and its anchor somewhere else, so their kings: 'Samlah of Masrekah' (Gen. 36:36), 'Shaul of Rehobot by the river' (Gen. 36:27), and: 'These are the kings who reigned in the land of Edom before any king reigned over the Israelites.'"
2. A. ["An estate may be gotten hastily at the beginning, but the end thereof shall not be blessed" (Prov. 20:21)]: "An estate may be gotten hastily at the beginning:" "These are the kings who reigned in the land of Edom before any king reigned over the Israelites."
    B. ". . . but the end thereof shall not be blessed:" "And saviors shall come up on mount Zion to judge the mount of Esau" (Obad. 1:21).

No. 1 contrasts the diverse origin of Roman rulers with the uniform origin of Israel's king in the house of David. No. 2 makes the same point still more forcefully. How so? Though Esau was the first to have kings, his land will eventually be overthrown (Freedman, p. 766, n. 3). So the point is that Israel will have kings after Esau no longer does, and the verse at hand is made to point to the end of Rome, a striking revision to express the importance in Israel's history to events in the lives of the patriarchs.

The final passage once more stresses the correspondence between Israel's and Edom's governments, respectively. The reciprocal character of their histories is then stated in a powerful way, with the further implication that, when the one rules, the other waits. So now Israel waits, but it will rule. The same point is made in what follows, but the expectation proves acute and immediate.

LXXXIII:IV

3. A. "Magdiel and Iram: these are the chiefs of Edom, that is Esau, the father of Edom, according to their dwelling places in the land of their possession" (Gen. 36:42):

B.   On the day on which Litrinus came to the throne, there appeared to R. Ammi in a dream this message: "Today Magdiel has come to the throne."

C.   He said, "One more king is required for Edom [and then Israel's turn will come]."

4. A.   Said R. Hanina of Sepphoris, "Why was he called Iram? For he is destined to amass [a word using the same letters] riches for the king-messiah."

B.   Said R. Levi, "There was the case of a ruler in Rome who wasted the treasuries of his father. Elijah of blessed memory appeared to him in a dream. He said to him, 'Your fathers collected treasures and you waste them.'

C.   "He did not budge until he filled the treasuries again."

No. 3 presents once more the theme that Rome's rule will extend only for a foreordained and limited time, at which point the Messiah will come. No. 4 explains the meaning of the name Iram. The concluding statement also alleges that Israel's saints even now make possible whatever wise decisions Rome's rulers make. That forms an appropriate conclusion to the matter.

In accomplishing the prophetic task of their day the authorship of Genesis Rabbah has rewritten the history of the world as classified and defined by Israel, and the issues prove profoundly theological. They spoke to Israel, the Jewish people, with an inward exposition of the problems of Israel's salvation. History in the service of prophecy was framed by Midrash-exegesis as a new medium for theological discourse. Why that medium should have proved urgent in the fourth and early fifth centuries and not earlier is clear. What changed? The advent of Christianity to power, that is, to a political standing in the world, demanded a new mode of thought, and history supplied it. And Judaism, facing in a new way the old question of postponed salvation, followed suit. But, as we shall now see, the task was not solely to explain what was happening. It also was to show Israel what it must do, and in Leviticus Rabbah we find the instructions.

9
Leviticus Rabbah

THE RULES OF SOCIETY
SET FORTH BY REVELATION

The message of Leviticus Rabbah attaches itself to the book of Leviticus, as if that book had come from prophecy, interpreted history, and addressed the issue of salvation. But it came from the priesthood and spoke of sanctification. The paradoxical syllogism—the as-if reading, the opposite of how things seem—of the composers of Leviticus Rabbah therefore reaches simple formulation. In the very setting of sanctification we find the promise of salvation. In the topics of the cult and the priesthood we uncover the national and social issues of the moral life and redemptive hope of Israel. The repeated comparison and contrast of priesthood and prophecy, sanctification and salvation, turn out to produce a complement, which comes to most perfect union in the text at hand.

Nearly all of Leviticus Rabbah deals with the national, social condition of Israel, and this in three contexts: (1) Israel's setting in the history of the nations, (2) the character of the inner life of Israel itself, (3) the future history of Israel. So the biblical book that deals with the holy Temple now is shown to address the holy people. Leviticus really discusses not the consecration of the cult but the sanctification of the nation—its conformity to God's will, laid forth in the Torah, and God's rules. When we review the document as a whole and ask what is that something else that the base text is supposed to address, it turns out that the sanctification of the cult stands for the salvation of the nation. The nation now is like the cult then, the ordinary Israelite now like the priest then. The holy way of life lived now, through acts to which merit accrues, corresponds to the holy rites then. The process of metamorphosis is full, rich, complete. When everything stands for something else, the something else repeatedly turns out to be the nation.

We recall how the authorship of Sifra, reading the book of Leviticus, found in Scripture not so much doctrines as examples of the correct classification of things. But what if an authorship turned to the book of Leviticus not only for evidence about the proper ordering of things, but also for proof of theological propositions of public consequence? And what if that authorship sought within Scripture not natural philosophy but theological truth and solace? Then Scripture's very character, as a highly propositional writing, with its own rhetoric, logic, and topical and propositional program, intervened. Should not a theological document resting on Scripture make its mark as essentially paraphrase, rhetoric and proposition both? In Leviticus Rabbah we see how Midrash as prophecy yields something quite unanticipated, which is a highly propositional statement and argument: facts assembled in support of a proposition.

Utterly unlike the Mishnah and Sifra, Leviticus Rabbah nonetheless falls into the classification of a cogent composition, put together with purpose and intended as a whole and in the aggregate to bear a meaning and state a message. Like Sifra, it is the opposite of an anthology or miscellany, nor is it to be compared only to a scrapbook, made up of this and that. The framers of Leviticus Rabbah treat topics, not particular verses. They make generalizations which are freestanding. They express cogent propositions through extended compositions, not episodic ideas. The authorship so collects and arranges their materials that an abstract proposition emerges. That proposition is not expressed only or mainly through episodic restatements, assigned, as we saw in Genesis Rabbah, to an order established by a base text. Rather it emerges through a logic of its own. This authorship of Leviticus Rabbah makes the move from an essentially exegetical mode of logical discourse to a fundamentally philosophical mode, and this it does in quest of prophetic insight. It is the shift from discourse framed around an established (hence old) text to syllogistic argument organized around a proposed (hence new) theorem or proposition. What changes, therefore, is the way in which cogent thought takes place, as people move from discourse contingent on some prior principle of organization to discourse without relation to a ready-made program inherited from an earlier paradigm.

Accordingly, when we listen to the framers of Leviticus Rabbah, we see how statements in the document at hand thus become intelligible not contingently, that is, on the strength of an established text, but a priori, that is, on the basis of a deeper logic of meaning and an independent principle of rhetorical intelligibility. How so? Leviticus Rabbah is topical, not exegetical. Each of its thirty-seven *parashiyyot* pursues its given topic and develops points relevant to that topic. It is logical, in that discourse appeals to an underlying principle of composition and intelligibility, and that logic inheres in what is said. An anthology of statements about a single subject becomes a composition of theorems about that subject. With Leviticus Rabbah rabbis take up the problem of saying what they wish to say not in an exegetical, but in a syllogistic and freely discursive logic and rhetoric, and they do so for theological, not merely philosophical and systemic, purposes.

We examine in particular a major unit that makes a simple point: the equality of anointed priest and ordinary Israelites. The expiation demanded of the one is no greater than that of the other. Considering the importance of the anointed priest, the ceremony by which he attains office, the sanctity attached to his labor, we cannot miss the polemic. What the anointed priest does unwittingly will usually involve some aspect of the cult. When the community commits a sin unwittingly, it will not involve the cult but some aspect of the collective life of the people. The one is no more consequential than the other; the same penalty pertains to both. So the people and the priest stand on the same plane before God. And the further meaning of the verse of Job, then, cannot be missed. When God hides his face, in consequence of which the people suffer, it is for a just cause. No one can complain; God is long-suffering but in the end exacts penalties. And these will cover not unwitting sin, such as Leviticus knows, but deliberate sin, as with the generation of the Flood, Sodom, and the Ten Tribes. There would thus appear to be several layers of meaning in the exegetical construction, which we must regard as a sustained and unified one, a truly amazing achievement.

Leviticus Rabbah Parashah 5

V:I

1. A. "If it is the anointed priest who sins [thus bringing guilt on the people, then let him offer to the Lord for the sin which he has committed a young bull without blemish]" (Lev. 4:3).

   B. "When he is quiet, who can condemn? When he hides his face, who can set him right [RSV: behold him] [whether it be a nation or a man? that a godless man should not reign, that he should not ensnare the people]" (Job 34:29–30).

   C. R. Meir interpreted [the matter in this way:] "'When he is quiet'—in his world, 'when he hides his face'—in his world.

   D. "The matter may be compared to the case of a judge who draws a veil inside and so does not see what goes on outside.

   E. "So the people of the generation of the flood thought: 'The thick clouds cover him, so he will not see [what we do]'" (Job 22:14).

F. They said to him, "That's enough from you, Meir."

2. A. Another interpretation: "When he is quiet, who can condemn? When he hides his face, who can set him right?" (Job 34:29).

B. When he gave tranquility to the generation of the flood, who could come and condemn them?

C. What sort of tranquility did he give them? "Their children are established in their presence, and their offspring before their eyes. [Their houses are safe from fear, and no rod of God is upon them]" (Job 21:8).

D. R. Levi and rabbis:

E. R. Levi said, "A woman would get pregnant and give birth in three days. [How do we know it?] Here, the word 'established' is used, and elsewhere: 'Be established in three days' (Exod. 19:15). Just as the word 'established' used there involves a span of three days, so the word 'established' used here means three days."

F. Rabbis say, "In a single day a woman would get pregnant and give birth.

G. "Here, the word 'established' is used, and elsewhere: 'And be established in the morning' (Exod. 34:2). Just as the word 'established' stated there involves a single day, so the word 'established' used here involves a single day."

3. A. "And their offspring before their eyes"—for they saw children and grandchildren.

B. "They send forth their little ones like a flock [and their children dance]" (Job 21:11).

C. [The word for "children" means] "their young."

D. Said R. Levi, "In Arabia for children they use the word 'the young.'"

4. A. "And their children dance" (Job 21:11)—

B. ["they dance"] like devils.

C. That is in line with the following verse of Scripture: "And satyrs will dance there" (Isa. 13:21).

5. A. They say: When one of them would give birth by day, she would say to her son, "Go and bring me a flint, so I can cut your umbilical cord."

B. If she gave birth by night, she would say to her son, "Go and light a lamp for me, so I can cut your umbilical cord."

C. There was the following case: A woman gave birth by night and said to her son, "Go and light a lamp for me, so I can cut your umbilical cord."

D. [In Aramaic:] When he went out to fetch it, a devil, Ashmadon [Asmodeus], head of the spirits, met him. While the two were wrestling with one another, the cock crowed. [Ashmadon] said to him, "Go, boast to your mother that my time has run out, for if my time had not run out, I could have killed you."

E. He said to him, "Go, boast to your mother's mother that my mother had not cut my umbilical cord, for if my mother had cut my umbilical cord, I would have beaten you."

 F. This illustrates that which is said: "Their houses are safe from fear" (Job 21:9)—from destroying spirits.

6. A. "And no rod of God is upon them"—[for their houses are free from suffering].

 B. [And this further] illustrates that which is said: "[When he is quiet, who can condemn] when he hides his face, who can put him right" (Job 34:30).

 C. When [God] hides his face from them, who can come and say to him, "You have not done right."

 D. And how, indeed, did he hide his face from them? When he brought the flood on them.

 E. That is in line with the following verse of Scripture: "And he blotted out every living substance which was upon the face of the earth" (Gen. 7:23).

7. A. "Whether it be to a nation [or a man together]" (Job 34:29)—this refers to the generation of the flood.

 B. "Or to a man"—this refers to Noah.

 C. "Together"—he had to rebuild his world from one man, he had to rebuild his world from one nation.

On the surface, the sole point of contact between the base verse and the intersecting verse, Lev. 4:3 and Job 34:29–30, is in the uncited part of the passage of Job, "that he should not ensnare the people." The anointed priest has sinned and in so doing has brought guilt on the entire people. If, however, that is why the entire assembly of exegeses of Job has been inserted here, that theme plays no rule in making the collection of materials on Job. For at no point in the present unit (or in the next one) does the important segment of the passage of Job come under discussion. The interpretation of Job 34:29 in light of the story of the flood predominates here. No. 1 has Meir's view that the entire passage refers to God's failure to intervene, with special reference to the flood. No. 2 pursues the same line of thought. No. 3 illustrates the notion that their children "are established in their presence," and nos. 3 and 4 continue to spell out the phrase-by-phrase exegesis of the same verse. No. 5 pursues the same line of thought. No. 6 shifts the ground of interpretation. Now God is "quiet," but later, in "hiding his face," he brings punishment on them. No. 7 completes the exegesis of the cited passage of Job in line with the view that Job was a contemporary of Noah and spoke of his ties. Noah might then serve as the counterpart and opposite of the priest who brings guilt on the people. But that is by no means the clear intent of the passage at hand.

V:II

1. A. Another interpretation: "When he is quiet, who can condemn?" (Job 34:29).

   B. When he gave tranquility to the Sodomites, who could come and condemn them?

   C. What sort of tranquility did he give them?

   D. "As for the earth, out of it comes bread, but underneath it is turned up as by fire. Its stones are the place of sapphires, and it has dust of gold" (Job 28:5–6).

2. A. "That path no bird of prey knows, and the falcon's eye has not seen it" (Job 28:7).

   B. R. Levi in the name of R. Yohanan bar Shahina: "The falcon [*bar hadayya* bird] spots its prey at a distance of eighteen miles."

   C. And how much is its portion [of food]?

   D. R. Meir said, "[A mere] two handbreadths."

   E. R. Judah said, "One handbreadth."

   F. R. Yosé said, "Two or three fingerbreadths."

   G. [In Aramaic:] And when it stood on the trees of Sodom, it could not see the ground because of the density of [the foliage of] the trees.

3. A. "When he hides his face, who can put him right?"

   B. When he hid his face from them, who comes to say to him, "You did not do rightly"?

   C. And when did he hide his face from them?

   D. When he made brimstone and fire rain down on them.

   E. That is in line with the following verse of Scripture: "Then the Lord made brimstone and fire rain on Sodom and Gomorrah" (Gen. 19:24).

The second unit simply carries forward the exercise of reading Job 28:5ff., now in line with the story of Sodom and Gomorrah, rather than the generation of the Flood. The message is being delivered through examples. But we are not in doubt as to the proposition.

V:III

1. A. Another interpretation of "When he is quiet, who can condemn? When he hides his face, who can set him right?" (Job 34:29).

   B. When he gave tranquility to the ten tribes, who could come and condemn them?

   C. What sort of tranquility did he give them? "Woe to those who are at ease in Zion, and to those who feel secure on the mountain of Samaria, the notable men of the first of the nations, to whom the house of Israel is to come" (Amos 6:1).

2. A. "Woe to those who are at ease in Zion" refers to the tribe of Judah and Benjamin.

   B. "Those who feel secure on the mountain of Samaria" refers to the ten tribes.

   C.   "The notable men of the first of the nations" who derive from the two noteworthy names, Shem and Eber.

   D.   When the nations of the world eat and drink, they pass the time in nonsense talk, saying, "Who is a sage, like Balaam! Who is a hero, like Goliath! Who is rich, like Haman!"

   E.   And the Israelites come after them and say to them, "Was not Ahitophel a sage, Samson a hero, Korah rich?"

3. A.   "Pass over to Calneh and see [and thence go to Hamath the great, then go down to Gath of the Philistines. Are they better than these kingdoms? Or is their territory greater than your territory?]" (Amos 6:2).

   B.   [Calneh] refers to Ctesiphon.

   C.   "Hamath the great" refers to Hamath of Antioch.

   D.   "And go down to Gath of the Philistines" refers to the mounds of the Philistines.

   E.   "Are they better than these kingdoms? Or is their territory greater than your territory?"

   F.   "O you who put far away the evil day" (Amos 6:3) [refers to] the day on which they would go into exile.

4. A.   "And bring near the seat of violence?" (Amos 6:3). This refers to Esau.

   B.   "Did you bring yourselves near to sit next to violence"—this refers to Esau.

   C.   That is in line with the following verse of Scripture: "For the violence done to your brother Jacob [shame shall cover you]" (Obad. 1:40).

5. A.   "[Woe to] those who lie upon beds of ivory" (Amos 6:4)—on beds made of the elephant's tusk.

   B.   "And stink on their couches" (Amos 6:4)—who do stinking transgressions on their beds.

   C.   "Who eat lambs from the flock [and calves from the midst of the stall]" (Amos 6:4).

   D.   They say: When one of them wanted to eat a kid of the flock, he would have the whole flock brought before him, and he would stand over it and slaughter it.

   E.   When he wanted to eat a calf, he would bring the entire herd of calves before him and stand over it and slaughter it.

6. A.   "Who sing idle songs to the sound of the harp [and like David invent for themselves instruments of music]" (Amos 6:5).

   B.   [They would say that] David provided them with musical instruments.

7. A.   "Who drink wine in bowls" (Amos 6:6).

   B.   Rab, R. Yohanan, and rabbis:

   C.   Rab said, "It is a very large bowl" [using the Greek].

   D.   R. Yohanan said, "It was in small cups."

   E.   Rabbis say, "It was in cups with saucers attached."

F.   Whence did the wine they drink come?

G.   R. Aibu in the name of R. Hanina said, "It was wine from Pelugta, for the wine would entice (*pth*) the body."

H.   And rabbis in the name of R. Hanina said, "It was from Pelugta [separation], since, because of their wine drinking, the ten tribes were enticed [from God] and consequently sent into exile."

8.   A.   "And anoint themselves with the finest oils" (Amos 6:6).

B.   R. Judah b. R. Ezekiel said, "This refers to oil of unripe olives, which removes hair and smooths the body."

C.   R. Haninah said, "This refers to oil of myrrh and cinnamon."

9.   A.   And [in spite of] all this glory: "They are not grieved over the ruin of Joseph" (Amos 6:6).

B.   "Therefore they shall now be the first of those to go into exile [and the revelry of those who stretch themselves shall pass away]" (Amos 6:7).

C.   What is the meaning of "the revelry of those who stretch themselves"?

D.   Said R. Aibu, "They had thirteen public baths, one for each of the tribes, and one additional one for all of them together.

E.   "And all of them were destroyed, and only this one [that had served all of them] survived.

F.   "This shows how much lewdness was done with them."

10. A.   "When he hides his face, who can set him right?" (Job 34:29).

B.   When he hid his face from them, who then could come and say to him, "You did not do right"?

C.   How did he hide his face from them? By bringing against them Sennacherib, the king of Assyria.

D.   That is in line with the following verse of Scripture: "In the fourteenth year of King Hezekiah, Sennacherib, king of Assyria, came up [against all the fortified cities of Judah and took them]" (Isa. 36:1).

11. A.   What is the meaning of "and took them"?

B.   Said R. Abba b. R. Kahana, "Three divine decrees were sealed on that day.

C.   "The decree against the ten tribes was sealed, for them to fall into the hand of Sennacherib; the decree against Sennacherib was sealed, for him to fall into the hand of Hezekiah; and the decree of Shebna was sealed, to be smitten with leprosy.

12. A.   "Whether it be a nation [or a man]" (Job 34:29)—this refers to Sennacherib, as it is said, "For a nation has come up upon my land" (Joel 1:6).

B.   ". . . or a man" (Job 34:29)—this refers to Israel: "For you, my sheep, the sheep of my pasture, are a man" (Ezek. 34:31).

C.   "Together" (Job 34:29)—this refers to King Uzziah, who was smitten with leprosy.

D.   That is in line with the following verse of Scripture: "And Uzziah the King was a leper until the day he died" (2 Chron. 26:21).

13. A. [Margulies: What follows treats ". . . whether it be a nation or a man together" (Job 34:29):] Now the justice of the Holy One, blessed be he, is not like man's justice.

    B. A mortal judge may show favor to a community, but he will never show favor to an individual.

    C. But the Holy One, blessed be he, is not so. Rather: "If it is the anointed priest who sins [thus bringing guilt on the people,] then let him offer [for the sin which he has committed] a young bull [without blemish to the Lord as a sin-offering]" (Lev. 4:3–4).

    D. "[If the whole congregation of Israel commits a sin unwittingly, and the thing is hidden from the eyes of the assembly, and they do any one of the things which the Lord has commanded not to be done and are guilty, when the sin which they have committed becomes known,] the assembly shall offer a young bull for a sin-offering" (Lev. 4:13–14). [God exacts the same penalty from an individual and from the community, and does not distinguish the one from the other. The anointed priest and the community both become subject to liability for the same offering, a young bull.]

Finally, at no. 13, we come to the verse with which we began. And we find a clear point of contact between the base verse and the intersecting one, Job 34:29, as Margulies, editor of the Hebrew text, explains. Still, there is no clear reason for including a sustained exegesis of Amos 6:3ff. No. 1 completes the original exegesis by applying the cited verse to the ten tribes, first tranquil, then punished, as at V:I, II. 1.C then links Amos 6:1 to the present context. Once Amos 6:1 makes its appearance, we work through the elements of Amos 6:1–7. That massive interpolation encompasses nos. 2–9. No. 10 resumes where no. 1 left off. No. 11 is tacked on to 10.D, and then nos. 12 and 13 continue the exegesis in terms of Israelite history of Job 34:29. Then, as I said, no. 13 stands completely separate from all that has gone before in V:I-III.12. What then is the primary intent of the exegete? As I said at the outset, it is to emphasize the equality of anointed priest and ordinary Israelites. Now we proceed to a secondary expansion of the established proposition.

V:IV

1. A. Said R. Abbahu, "It is written, 'Take heed that you do not forsake the Levite [as long as you live in your land]' (Deut. 12:19). What follows thereafter? 'When the Lord your God enlarges your territory [as he has promised you]' (Deut. 12:20).

    B. "What has one thing got to do with the other?

    C. "Said the Holy One, blessed be he, 'In accord with your gifts will they enlarge your [place].'"

D. R. Huna in the name of R. Aha, "If a slave brings as his offering a
    young bull, while his master brings a lamb, the slave takes precedence
    over his master.

E. "This is in accord with what we have learned in the Mishnah: 'If the
    young bull of the anointed priest and the young bull of the commu-
    nity are waiting [sacrifice], the young bull of the anointed priest takes
    precedence over the young bull of the community in all aspects of the
    sacrificial rite'" (M. Hor. 3:6).

2. A. "A man's gift makes room for him and brings him before great men"
        (Prov. 18:16).

    B. There was the following case. R. Eliezer, R. Joshua, and R. Aqiba
        went to the harborside of Antioch to collect funds for the support of
        sages.

    C. [In Aramaic:] A certain Abba Yudan lived there.

    D. He would carry out his religious duty [of philanthropy] in a liberal
        spirit, but had lost his money. When he saw our masters, he went
        home with a sad face. His wife said to him, "What's wrong with you,
        that you look so sad?"

    E. He repeated the tale to her: "Our masters are here, and I don't know
        what I shall be able to do for them."

    F. His wife, who was a truly philanthropic woman—what did she say to
        him? "You only have one field left. Go, sell half of it and give them
        the proceeds."

    G. He went and did just that. When he was giving them the money, they
        said to him, "May the Omnipresent make up all your losses."

    H. Our masters went their way.

    I. He went out to plow. While he was plowing the half of the field that
        he had left, the Holy One, blessed be he, opened his eyes. The earth
        broke open before him, and his cow fell in and broke her leg. He went
        down to raise her up, and found a treasure beneath her. He said, "It
        was for my gain that my cow broke her leg."

    J. When our masters came back [in Aramaic:] they asked about a certain
        Abba Yudan and how he was doing. They said, "Who can gaze on the
        face of Abba Yudan [which glows with prosperity]—Abba Yudan, the
        owner of flocks of goats, Abba Yudan, the owner of herds of asses,
        Abba Yudan, the owner of herds of camels."

    K. He came to them and said to them, "Your prayer in my favor has
        produced returns and returns on the returns."

    L. They said to him, "Even though someone else gave more than you
        did, we wrote your name at the head of the list."

    M. Then they took him and sat him next to themselves and recited in his
        regard the following verse of Scripture: "A man's gift makes room for
        him and brings him before great men" (Prov. 18:16).

3. A. R. Hiyya bar Abba called for charity contributions in support of a school in Tiberias. A member of the household of Siloni got up and pledged a litra of gold.
   B. R. Hiyya bar Abba took him and sat him next to himself and recited in his regard the following verse of Scripture: "A man's gift makes room for him and brings him before great men" (Prov. 18:16).
4. A. [In Aramaic:] R. Simeon b. Laqish went to Bosrah. A certain Abba [Lieberman deletes: Yudan], "the Deceiver," lived there. It was not— Heaven forfend—that he really was a deceiver. Rather, he would practice [holy] deception in doing the religious duty [of philanthropy].
   B. [In Aramaic:] He would see what the rest of the community would pledge, and he would then pledge to take upon himself [a gift equivalent to that of the rest of the] community.
   C. R. Simeon b. Laqish took him and sat him next to himself and recited in his regard the following verse of Scripture: "A man's gift makes room for him and brings him before great men" (Prov. 18:16).

We find neither a base verse nor an intersecting one, such as characterized V:I-III. Rather, what will be the secondary verse—Prov. 18:16— comes in the distant wake of a problem presented by the information of Lev. 4. Specifically, we find reference to the sacrifice of the young bulls of the high priest, of the community, and of the ruler. The issue, then, naturally arises, which one comes first? The Mishnah answers that question, at M. Hor. 3:6.

Reflection upon that answer generates the observation that the anointed priest comes first, as in Scripture's order, in particular when the offerings are of the same value. But if one offering is more valuable than the other, the more valuable offering takes precedence. Then comes secondary reflection on the fact that a person's gift establishes his rank even if it is on other grounds lower than what he otherwise would attain. No. 1 does not pursue that secondary reflection, but invites it at 1.C. The invocation of Prov. 18:16, then, is not on account of Lev. 4 at all. It must follow that nos. 2–4 would better serve a compilation of materials on Deut. 12:19–20 than the present passage. What follows no. 1 serves a purpose in no way closely connected either to the sense or to the syntax of our passage. The entire complex, nos. 2–4, occurs at Y. Hor. 3:4. It is lifted whole, attached because of the obvious relevance to no. 1. We find no pretense, then, that these stories relate in any way to Lev. 4. For the storyteller at no. 2, the climax comes at L-M, the sages' recognition that their placing of Abba Yudan at the head of the list had made possible the serendipitous accident. Nos. 3 and 4 omit the miraculous aspect entirely.

V:V

1. A. Reverting to the base text: "If it is the anointed priest who sins" (Lev. 4:3).
    B. This refers to Shebna.
2. A. "[Thus says the Lord, God of hosts] 'Come, go to this steward (*skn*), to Shebna, who is over the household [and say to him, 'What have you to do here and whom have you here, that you have hewn here a tomb for yourself, you who hew a tomb on the height and carve a habitation for yourself in the rock? Behold, the Lord will hurl you away violently, O you strong young man! He will seize firm hold on you, and whirl you round and round and throw you like a ball into a wide land; there you shall die, and there shall be your splendid chariots, you shame of your master's house. I will thrust you from your office and you will be cast down from your station]" (Isa. 22:15–19).
    B. R. Eliezer said, "He was a high priest."
    C. R. Judah b. Rabbi said, "He was steward."
    D. In the view of R. Eliezer, who said he was a high priest [we may bring evidence from Scripture] for it is written, "And I will clothe him with your robe [and will bind your girdle on him and will commit your authority into his hand]" (Isa. 22:21).
    E. In the view of R. Judah b. Rabbi, who said he was steward, [we may bring evidence from Scripture] for it is written, "And I will commit your authority to his hand" (Isa. 22:21).
    F. R. Berekiah said, "What is a 'steward'? It is one who comes from Sikhni."
3. A. And he went up and was appointed *komes opsarion* [the Greek for chief cook] in Jerusalem.
    B. That is in line with the prophet's condemnation, saying to him, "What have you to do here, and whom have you here?" (Isa. 22:16).
    C. "You exile, son of an exile! What wall have you built here, what pillar have you put up here, and what nail have you hammered in here?!"
    D. R. Eleazar said, "A person has to have a nail or a peg firmly set in a synagogue so as to have the right to be buried in that place [in which he is living]."
    E. "And have you hewn here a tomb for yourself?" (Isa. 22:16). He made himself a kind of a dovecot and put his tomb on top of it.
    F. "You who hew a tomb on the height" (Isa. 22:16)—
    G. R. Ishmael in the name of Mar Uqba, "On the height the decree was hewn out concerning him, indicating that he should not have a burial place in the land of Israel."
    H. "You who carve a habitation for yourself in the rock" (Isa. 22:16)—a stone coffin.
    I. "Behold, the Lord will hurl you away violently" (Isa. 22:17)—one rejection after another.

J. ". . . hurl away violently (*gbr*)"—[since the word *gbr* also means cock:] said R. Samuel b. R. Nahman [in Aramaic:], "it may be compared to a cock which is driven and goes from place to place."

K. "He will seize a firm hold on you" (Isa. 22:17) [since the words for "firm hold" may also be translated "wrap around," thus: "And he will wrap you around"] the meaning is that he was smitten with *saraat* [leprosy] in line with that which you find in Scripture, "And he will wrap his lip around" (Lev. 13:45).

L. "And whirl you round and round [and throw you like a ball]" (Isa. 22:18)—exile after exile.

M. "Like a ball"—just as a ball is caught from hand to hand and does not fall to the ground, so [will it be for him].

N. "Into a wide land"—this means Casiphia (Ezra 8:17).

O. "There you shall die and there shall be your splendid chariots" (Isa. 22:18).

4. A. In accord with the position of R. Eliezer, who said that Shebna had been a high priest [the reference to the splendid chariots implies] that he had been deriving personal benefit from the offerings.

B. In accord with the view of R. Judah b. Rabbi, who said that he had been steward [the reference to the splendid chariots implies] that he had derived personal benefit from things that had been consecrated for use in the upkeep of the sanctuary.

C. "You shame of your master's house" (Isa. 22:18).

D. In accord with the position of R. Eliezer, who said that Shebna had been a high priest, [the shame was] that he had treated the offerings in a disgraceful way.

E. In accord with the view of R. Judah b. Rabbi, who said that he had been steward, [the shame was] that he had treated both of his masters disgracefully, that is Hezekiah, on the one side, Isaiah on the other.

5. A. R. Berekhiah in the name of R. Abba b. R. Kahana: "What did Shebna and Joahaz [2 Kings. 18:18] do? They wrote a message and attached it to an arrow and shot it to Sennacherib through the window. In the message was written the following: "We and everyone in Jerusalem want you, but Hezekiah and Isaiah don't want you."

B. Now this is just what David had said [would happen]: "For lo, the wicked bend the bow, they have fitted their arrow to the string" (Ps. 11:2).

C. "For lo, the wicked bend the bow"—this refers to Shebna and Joahaz.

D. "They have fitted their arrow to the string"—on the bowstring.

E. "To shoot in the dark at the upright in heart" (Ps. 11:2)—at two upright in heart, Hezekiah and Isaiah.

What the exegete contributes to the explanation of Lev. 4:3 is simply the example of how an anointed priest may sin. The rest of the passage is a systematic exposition of the verses about Shebna. But the entire matter of Shebna belongs here only within Eliezer's opinion that he was a high priest. That is a rather remote connection to the present passage of Leviticus. So because of the allegation that Shebna was high priest, the entire passage—fully worked out on its own—was inserted here. The redactor then appeals to theme, not to content, in drawing together the cited verses of Leviticus and Isaiah. Nos. 2 and 4 are continuous with one another. No. 3 inserts a systematic, phrase-by-phrase exegesis of Isa. 22:15ff. No. 5 then complements the foregoing with yet further relevant material. So the construction, apart from no. 1, is cogent and well conceived. Only linkage to Lev. 4:3 is farfetched.

V:VI

1. A. "If it is the anointed priest who sins" (Lev. 4:3).
   B. [What follows occurs at T. Hor. 2:4, explaining M. Hor. 3:4, cited above at V:IV.1.E:] [If] the anointed high priest must atone [for a sin] and the community must be atoned for [in line with Lev. 4:13], it is better that the one who [has the power to] make atonement take precedence over the one for whom atonement is made,
   C. as it is written, "And he will atone for himself and for his house" (Lev. 16:17).
   D. ["His house"] refers to his wife.
2. A. "If it is the anointed priest who sins" (Lev. 4:3)—
   B. Will an anointed priest commit a sin!
   C. Said R. Levi, "Pity the town whose physician has gout [and cannot walk to visit the sick], whose governor has one eye, and whose public defender plays the prosecutor in capital cases."
3. A. "[If it is the anointed priest who sins] thus bringing guilt [on the people, then let him offer for the sin which he has committed a young bull . . .]" (Lev. 4:3).
   B. Said R. Isaac, "It is a case of death by burning [inflicted on one who commits sacrilege by consuming offerings from the altar]."
   C. "The matter may be compared to the keeper of a bear, who ate up the rations of the bear. The king said, 'Since he went and ate up the bear's rations, let the bear eat him.'
   D. "So does the Holy One, blessed be he, say, 'Since Shebna enjoyed benefit from things that had been consecrated to the altar [for burning], let fire consume him.'"
4. A. Said R. Aibu, "Once there was a butcher in Sepphoris, who fed Israelites carrion and torn meat. On the eve of the Day of Atonement he went out drinking and got drunk. He climbed up to the roof of his house and fell off and died. The dogs began to lick him.
   B. "[In Aramaic:] They came and asked R. Hanina the law about moving his corpse away from the dogs [on the Day of Atonement].
   C. "He said to him, 'You will be holy people to me, therefore you shall

not eat any meat that is torn of beasts in the field, you shall cast it to the dogs' (Exod. 22:30).

D. "'This man robbed from the dogs and fed carrion and torn meat to Israelites. Leave him to them. They are eating what belongs to them.'"

5. A. "He shall bring the bull to the door of the tent of meeting before the Lord [and lay his hand on the head of the bull and kill the bull before the Lord]" (Lev. 4:4).

    B. Said R. Isaac, "The matter may be compared to the case of a king, one of whose admirers paid him honor by giving him a handsome gift and by offering him lovely words of praise. The king then said, 'Set this gift at the gate of the palace, so that everyone who comes and goes may see [and admire] it,'

    C. "as it is said, 'And he shall bring the bull [to the door of the tent of meeting].'"

The opening units, nos. 1–4, form a kind of appendix of miscellanies to what has gone before. No. 1 reaches back to V:IV, explaining the passage of the Mishnah cited there. No. 2 is joined to no. 3, which relates to the cited passage to Shebna. So nos. 2 and 3 complete the discussion of V:V. It seems to me that no. 4 is attached to no. 3 as an illustration of the case of a public official who abuses his responsibility. No. 5 provides a fresh point, moving on to a new verse. There is no intersecting verse; the exegesis is accomplished solely through a parable.

V:VII

1. A. "[If the whole congregation of Israel commits a sin unwittingly and the thing is hidden from the eyes of the assembly, and they do any one of the things which the Lord has commanded not to be done and are guilty, when the sin which they have committed becomes known, the assembly shall offer a young bull for a sin-offering and bring it before the tent of meeting;] and the elders of the congregation shall lay their hands [upon the head of the bull before the Lord]" (Lev. 4:13–15).

    B. [Since, in laying their hands (*smk*) on the head of the bull, the elders sustain (*smk*) the community by adding to it the merit they enjoy] said R. Isaac, "The nations of the world have none to sustain them, for it is written, 'And those who sustain Egypt will fall" (Ezek. 30:6).

    C. "But Israel has those who sustain it, as it is written: 'And the elders of the congregation shall lay their hands [and so sustain Israel] (Lev. 4:15).'"

2. A. Said R. Eleazar, "The nations of the world are called a congregation, and Israel is called a congregation.

    B. "The nations of the world are called a congregation: 'For the congregation of the godless shall be desolate' (Job 15:34).

C. "And Israel is called a congregation: 'And the elders of the congregation shall lay their hands' (Lev. 4:15).

D. "The nations of the world are called sturdy bulls and Israel is called sturdy bulls.

E. "The nations of the world are called sturdy bulls: 'The congregation of [sturdy] bulls with the calves of the peoples' (Ps. 68:31).

F. "Israel is called sturdy bulls, as it is said, 'Listen to me, you sturdy [bullish] of heart' (Isa. 46:13).

G. "The nations of the world are called excellent, and Israel is called excellent.

H. "The nations of the world are called excellent: 'You and the daughters of excellent nations' (Exod. 32:18).

I. "Israel is called excellent: 'They are the excellent, in whom is all my delight' (Ps. 16:4).

J. "The nations of the world are called sages, and Israel is called sages.

K. "The nations of the world are called sages: 'And I shall wipe out sages from Edom' (Obad. 1:8).

L. "And Israel is called sages: 'Sages store up knowledge' (Prov. 10:14).

M. "The nations of the world are called unblemished, and Israel is called unblemished.

N. "The nations of the world are called unblemished: 'Unblemished as are those that go down to the pit' (Prov. 1:12).

O. "And Israel is called unblemished: 'The unblemished will inherit goodness' (Prov. 28:10).

P. "The nations of the world are called men, and Israel is called men.

Q. "The nations of the world are called men: 'And you men who work iniquity' (Ps. 141:4).

R. "And Israel is called men: 'To you who are men I call' (Prov. 8:4).

S. "The nations of the world are called righteous, and Israel is called righteous.

T. "The nations of the world are called righteous: 'And righteous men shall judge them' (Ez. 23:45).

U. "And Israel is called righteous: 'And your people—all of them are righteous' (Isa. 60:21).

V. "The nations of the world are called mighty, and Israel is called mighty.

W. "The nations of the world are called mighty: 'Why do you boast of evil, O mighty man' (Ps. 52:3).

X. "And Israel is called mighty: 'Mighty in power, those who do his word'" (Ps. 103:20).

We see two distinct types of exegeses, one to which the base passage is central, the other to which it is peripheral. Yet the two passages belong together, and we have every reason to suppose that they were made up as a single cogent statement. No. 1 focuses upon the double meaning of the word *smk*, one, lay hands, the other, sustain, drawing the contrast stated by Isaac. Once such a contrast is drawn, a catalogue of eight further contrasts will be laid out. Since the opening set, 2.A-B, depends upon the passage at hand, we must accept the possibility that Eleazar's statement has been constructed to work its way through the contrast established by Isaac.

Both authorities make the same point. Even though the nations of the world are subject to the same language as is applied to Israel, they still do not fall into the same classification. For language is dual. When a word applies to Israel, it serves to praise, and when the same word applies to the nations, it underlines their negative character. Both are called congregation, but the nations' congregation is desolate, and so throughout, as the context of the passage cited concerning the nations repeatedly indicates. The nations' sages are wiped out; the unblemished nations go down to the pit; the nations, called men, only work iniquity. Now that is precisely the contrast drawn in Isaac's saying, so, as I said, the whole should be deemed a masterpiece of unitary composition. Then the two types of exegesis—direct, peripheral—turn out to complement one another, each making its own point.

V:VIII

1. A. R. Simeon b. Yohai taught, "How masterful are the Israelites, for they know how to find favor with their creator."

   B. Said R. Yudan [in Aramaic:], "It is like the case of Samaritan [beggars]. The Samaritan [beggars] are clever at begging. One of them goes to a housewife, saying to her, 'Do you have an onion? Give it to me.' After she gives it to him, he says to her, 'Is there such a thing as an onion without bread?' After she gives him [bread], he says to her, 'Is there such a thing as food without drink?' So, all in all, he gets to eat and drink."

   C. Said R. Aha [in Aramaic:], "There is a woman who knows how to borrow things, and there is a woman who does not. The one who knows how to borrow goes over to her neighbor. The door is open, but she knocks [anyhow]. Then she says to her neighbor, 'Greetings, good neighbor. How're you doing? How's your husband doing? How're your kids doing? Can I come in? [By the way], would you have such-and-such a utensil? Would you lend it to me? [The neighboring housewife] says to her, 'Yes, of course.'

   D. "But the one who does not know how to borrow goes over to her neighbor. The door is closed, so she just opens it. She says [to the neighboring housewife], 'Do you have such-and-such a utensil?

Would you lend it to me?' [The neighboring housewife] says to her, 'No.'"

E. Said R. Hunia [in Aramaic:], "There is a tenant farmer who knows how to borrow things, and there is a tenant farmer who does not know how to borrow. The one who knows how to borrow combs his hair, brushes off his clothes, puts on a good face, and then goes over to the overseer of his work to borrow from him. [The overseer] says to him, 'How's the land doing?' He says to him, 'May you have the merit of being fully satisfied with its [wonderful] produce.' 'How are the oxen doing?' He says to him, 'May you have the merit of being fully satisfied with their fat.' 'How are the goats doing?' 'May you have the merit of being fully satisfied with their young.' 'And what would you like?' Then he says, 'Now if you might have an extra ten denars, would you give them to me?' The overseer replies, 'If you want, take twenty.'

F. "But the one who does not know how to borrow leaves his hair a mess, his clothes filthy, his face gloomy. He too goes over to the overseer to borrow from him. The overseer says to him, 'How's the land doing?' He replies, 'I hope it will produce at least what [in seed] we put into it.' 'How are the oxen doing?' 'They're scrawny.' 'How are the goats doing?' 'They're scrawny too.' 'And what do you want?' 'Now if you might have an extra ten denars, would you give them to me?' The overseer replies, 'Go, pay me back what you already owe me!'"

G. Said R. Hunia, "David was one of the good tenant farmers. To begin with, he starts a psalm with praise [of God], saying, 'The heavens declare the glory of God, and the firmament shows his handiwork' (Ps. 19:2). The Heaven says to him, 'Perhaps you need something?' 'The firmament shows his handiwork.' The firmament says to him, 'Perhaps you need something?'

H. "And so he would continue to sing: 'Day unto day utters speech, and night to night reveals knowledge' (Ps. 19:3).

I. "Said to him the Holy One, blessed be he, 'What do you want?'

J. "He said before him, 'Who can discern errors?' (Ps. 19:13).

K. "'What sort of unwitting sin have I done before you?'

L. "[God] said to him, 'Lo, this one is remitted, and that one is forgiven you.'

M. "'And cleanse me of hidden sins' (Ps. 19:13). '. . . from the secret sins that I have done before you.'

N. "He said to him, 'Lo, this one is remitted, and that one is forgiven to you.'

O. "'Keep back your servant also from deliberate ones.' This refers to transgressions done in full knowledge.

P. "'That they may not have dominion over me. Then I shall be faultless' (Ps. 19:14). This refers to the most powerful of transgressions.

Q. "'And I shall be clear of great transgression'" (Ps. 19:14).
R. Said R. Levi, "David said before the Holy One, blessed be he, 'Lord of the age[s], you are a great God, and, as for me, my sins are great too. It will take a great God to remit and forgive great sins: For your name's sake, O Lord, pardon my sin, for [your name] is great (Ps. 25:11).'"

Once more the construction appears from beginning to end to aim at a single goal. The opening statement, 1.A, makes the point, and the closing construction, Gff., illustrates it. In the middle come three apt narratives serving as similes, all told in Aramaic, and all following exactly the same pattern. Then the systematic account of a passage of Scripture is provided to make exactly the same point. I cannot state the exact sense of the passage on the heaven and the firmament, G, but from that point, the discourse is pellucid. Q-R should be separated from G-P, since what Levi's statement does is simply augment the primary passage. The unity of theme and conception accounts for the drawing together of the entire lot. To be sure, B-F can serve other purposes. But since Hunia's statement, E-F, introduces his exegesis of Ps. 19, the greater likelihood is that a single hand has produced the entire matter (possibly excluding Q-R) to make a single point. Why has the redactor thought the passage appropriate here? The offering for unwitting sin of Lev. 4, to which K makes reference in the progression through the types of sins, from minor to major, for which David seeks forgiveness, certainly accounts for the inclusion of the whole. Then whoever made up the passage did not find the stimulus in Lev. 4. For the rather general observation of 1.A states the framer's message. That message pertains to diverse contexts, as the exposition of Ps. 19 makes clear; nothing would compel someone to make up a passage of this sort to serve Lev. 4 in particular.

We deal with a highly formalized mode of setting forth scriptural exegesis. I see two important forms. The paramount and dominant exegetical construction is the base verse/intersecting verse exegesis. In such an exercise, we read one thing in terms of something else. To begin with, it is the base verse in terms of the intersecting verse. But, as the reader will have observed in the text itself, it also is the intersecting verse in other terms as well—a multiple layered construction of analogy and parable. The intersecting verse's elements always turn out to stand for, to signify, to speak of, something other than that to which they openly refer. If water stands for Torah, the skin disease for evil speech, the reference to something for some other thing entirely, then the mode of thought at hand is simple. One thing symbolizes another, speaks not of itself but of some other thing entirely. This we may call an "as-if way" of seeing things. That is to say, it is *as if* a common object or symbol really represented an uncommon one. Nothing says what it means.

Everything important speaks metonymically, elliptically, parabolically, symbolically. All statements carry deeper meaning, which inheres in other statements altogether. The profound sense, then, of the base verse emerges only through restatement within and through the intersecting verse—as if the base verse spoke of things that, on the surface, we do not see at all. Accordingly, if we ask the single prevalent literary construction to testify to the prevailing frame of mind, its message is that things are never what they seem. All things demand interpretation. Interpretation begins in the search for analogy, for that to which the thing is likened, hence the deep sense in which all exegesis at hand is parabolic. It is a quest for that for which the thing in its deepest structure stands. This is where Midrash as prophecy shades over into Midrash as parable.

And that brings us to a clear picture of what makes Midrash a model for ourselves. In Midrash-exegesis, the basic hermeneutics consists in an exercise in analogical thinking. That is to say, if something is like something else, in Leviticus Rabbah, it stands for, evokes, or symbolizes that which is quite outside itself. It may be the opposite of something else, in which case in the Mishnah it follows the opposite rule, and in the case of Leviticus Rabbah it conforms to the exact opposite of the rules that govern that something else. The reasoning is analogical or it is contrastive, and the fundamental logic is taxonomic. The taxonomy rests on those comparisons and contrasts we should call, as I said, metonymic and parabolic. In that case what lies on the surface misleads. What lies beneath or beyond the surface—there is the true reality, the world of truth and meaning. To revert to the issue of taxonomy, the tracts that allow classification serve only for that purpose. How shall we characterize people who see things this way? They constitute the opposite of ones who call a thing as it is. Self-evidently, they have become accustomed to perceiving more—or less—than is at hand. Perhaps that is a natural mode of thought for the Jews of this period (and not then alone), so long used to calling themselves God's first love, yet now seeing others with greater worldly reason claiming that same advantaged relationship.

This draws us toward the theological discourse undertaken in the document before us. For it is not in mind only, but still more, in the politics of the world, that the people that remembered its origins along with the very creation of the world and founding of humanity, that recalled how it alone served, and serves, the one and only God, for more than three hundred years, had confronted a quite different existence.

The radical disjuncture between the way things were and the way Scripture said things were supposed to be—and in actuality would some day become—surely imposed an unbearable tension. It was one thing for the slave born to slavery to endure. It was another for the free man sold into slavery to accept that same condition. The vanquished people, the nation that had lost its city and its temple, that had, moreover, produced another nation from its midst to take over its Scripture and much else could not bear too much reality. That defeated people will then have found refuge in a mode of thought that trained vision to see other things otherwise than as the eyes perceived them. Among the diverse ways by which the weak and subordinated accommodate to their circumstance, the one of iron-willed pretense in life is most likely to yield the mode of thought at hand: things never are, because they cannot be, what they seem.

In this context we note in the case before us, as in numerous other passages in this writing, the recurrence of a list of events in Israel's history, meaning, in this context, Israel's history solely in scriptural times, down through the return to Zion. The one-time events of the generation of the Flood, Sodom and Gomorrah, the patriarchs and the sojourn in Egypt, the exodus, the revelation of the Torah at Sinai, the golden calf, the Davidic monarchy and the building of the Temple, Sennacherib, Hezekiah, and the destruction of northern Israel, Nebuchadnezzar and the destruction of the Temple in 586, the life of Israel in Babylonian captivity, Daniel and his associates, Mordecai and Haman— these events occur over and over again. They turn out to serve as paradigms of sin and atonement, steadfastness and divine intervention, and equivalent lessons. We find, in fact, a fairly standard repertoire of scriptural heroes or villains, on the one side, and conventional lists of Israel's enemies and their actions and downfall, on the other. The boastful, for instance, include the generation of the Flood, Sodom and Gomorrah, Pharaoh, Sisera, Sennacherib, Nebuchadnezzar, the wicked empire (Rome)—contrasted to Israel, "despised and humble in this world." The four kingdoms recur again and again, always ending, of course, with Rome, with the repeated message that after Rome will come Israel. But Israel has to make this happen through its faith and submission to God's will. Lists of enemies ring the changes on Cain, the Sodomites, Pharaoh, Sennacherib, Nebuchadnezzar, Haman.

These lists, then, through the power of repetition make a single enormous point or prove a social law of history—hence, again, Midrash as prophecy. The catalogues of exemplary heroes and historical events serve a further purpose. They provide a model of how contemporary events are to be absorbed into the biblical paradigm. Since biblical events exemplify recurrent happenings, sin and redemption, forgiveness and atonement, they lose their one-time character. At the same time and in the same way, current events find a place within the ancient, but eternally present, paradigmatic scheme. So no new historical events, other than exemplary episodes in lives of heroes, demand narration because, through what is said about the past, what was happening in the times of the framers of Leviticus Rabbah would also come under consideration. This mode of dealing with biblical history and contemporary events produces two reciprocal effects. The first is the mythicization of biblical stories, their removal from the framework of ongoing, unique patterns of history and sequences of events, and their transformation into accounts of things that happen all the time. The second is that contemporary events too lose all their specificity and enter the paradigmatic framework of established mythic existence. So the Scripture's myth happens every day, and every day produces reenactment of the Scripture's myth.

At the center of the pretense, that is, the as-if mentality of Leviticus Rabbah and its framers, we find a simple proposition. Israel is God's special love. That love is shown in a simple way. Israel's present condition of subordination derives from its own deeds. It follows that God cares, so Israel may look forward to redemption on God's part in response to Israel's own regeneration through repentance. When the exegetes proceeded to open the scroll of Leviticus, they found numerous occasions to state that proposition in concrete terms and specific contexts. Sinners bring on their own sickness. But God heals through that very ailment. The nations of the world govern in heavy succession, but Israel's lack of faith guaranteed their rule and its moment of renewal will end it. Israel's leaders—priests, prophets, kings—fall into an entirely different category from those of the nations, as much as does Israel. In these and other concrete allegations, the same classical message comes forth. At the end we must ask how systemic theology is worked out through exegetical form, since, we see, the document does not express these syllogisms in the form of arguments at all. Rather they come before us as statements of fact, and the facts upon which numerous statements rest derive from Scripture. The appeal is to an autonomous realm, namely, reason confirmed by experience. The repeated claim is not that things are so merely because Scripture says what it says, but that things happened as they happened in accord with laws we may verify or test (as Scripture, among other sources of facts, tells us). The emphasis is on the sequence of events, the interrelationship exhibited by them. How does Scripture in particular participate? It is not *in particular* at all.

Scripture serves as a source of information, much as any history of the world or of a nation would provide sources of information: facts. The conditional syllogisms of our composition over and over again run through the course of history. The effort is to demonstrate that the rule at hand applies at all times, under all circumstances. It is because the conditional syllogism must serve under all temporal circumstances. The recurrent listing of events subject to a single rule runs as often as possible through the course of all human history, from creation to the fourth monarchy (Rome), which, everyone knows, is the end of time prior to the age that is coming. Accordingly, the veracity of rabbinic conditional arguments depends over and over again on showing that the condition holds at all times. The facts with which our authorship has worked are scriptural. The propositions they propose to demonstrate through these facts, however, are eternal. That is why they found in exegesis the correct structure for the presentation of their theology.

10
Pesiqta deRab Kahana

THE RULES OF THE HOLY WAY OF LIFE
SET FORTH BY REVELATION

Pesiqta deRab Kahana is a Midrash-compilation that appeals for its themes and lections to the liturgical calendar. Unlike Genesis Rabbah and Leviticus Rabbah, the document focuses upon the life of the synagogue. Its framers set forth propositions in the manner of the authorship of Leviticus Rabbah, but these are framed by appeal not only to the rules governing the holy society, as in Leviticus Rabbah, but also to the principal events of Israel's history, celebrated in the worship of the synagogue. What we do not find in this Midrash-compilation is exposition of pentateuchal or prophetic passages, verse by verse, or the presentation of syllogisms arranged in accord with either pentateuchal or prophetic passages. The basis chosen by our authorship for organizing and setting forth its propositions is rather the character and theme of a holy day.

The contrast to the earlier compilations—this one is generally assigned to ca. 500—is striking. The framers of Sifra and Sifré to Numbers and Sifré to Deuteronomy follow the verses of Scripture and attach to them whatever messages they wish to deliver. The authorship of Genesis Rabbah follows suit, though less narrowly guided by verses and more clearly interested in their broader themes. The framers of Leviticus Rabbah attached rather broad, discursive and syllogistic statements to verses of the book of Leviticus, but these verses do not follow in close sequence, one, then the next, as in Sifra and its friends. That program of exposition of verses of Scripture read in or out of sequence, of organization of discourse in line with biblical books, parallel to the Tosefta's and Talmuds' authorships' exposition of passages of the Mishnah, read in close sequence or otherwise, we see, defines what our authorship has not done. Here, by contrast, all the selected base verses, pentateuchal or prophetic, are in other documents of the same time and place identified with synagogal lections for specified holy days, special Sabbaths or festivals.

These synagogal discourses form a coherent statement. I see these three propositions. First, God loves Israel, that love is unconditional, and Israel's response to God must be obedience to the religious duties that God has assigned, which will produce merit. Israel's obedience to God is what will save Israel. That means doing the religious duties as required by the Torah, which is the mark of God's love for—and regeneration of—Israel. The tabernacle symbolizes the union of Israel and God. When Israel does what God asks above, Israel will prosper down below. If Israel remembers Amalek down below, God will remember Amalek up above and will wipe him out. A mark of Israel's loyalty to God is remembering Amalek. God does not require the animals that are sacrificed, since man could never match God's appetite, if that were the issue, but the savor pleases God [as a mark of Israel's loyalty and obedience]. The first sheaf returns to God God's fair share of the gifts that God bestows on Israel, and those who give it benefit, while those who hold it back suffer. Observing religious duties, typified by the rites of the festival, brings a great reward of the merit that ultimately leads to redemption. God's ways are just, righteous and merciful, as shown by God's concern that the offspring remain with the mother for seven days. God's love for Israel is so intense that he wants to hold them back for an extra day after the festival in order to spend more time with them, because, unlike the nations of the world, Israel knows how to please God. This is a mark of God's love for Israel.

Second, God is reasonable and when Israel has been punished, it is in accord with God's rules. God forgives penitent Israel and is abundant in mercy. The good and the wicked die in exactly the same circumstance or condition. Laughter is vain because it is mixed with grief. A wise person will not expect too much joy. But when people suffer, there ordinarily is a good reason for it. That is only one sign that God is reasonable and God never did anything lawless and wrong to Israel or made unreasonable demands, and there was, therefore, no reason for Israel to lose confidence in God or to abandon him. God punished Israel, to be sure. But this was done with reason. Nothing happened to Israel of which God did not give fair warning in advance, and Israel's failure to heed the prophets brought about its fall. And God will forgive a faithful Israel. Even though the Israelites sinned by making the golden calf, God forgave them and raised them up. On the New Year, God executes justice, but the justice is tempered with mercy. The rites of the New

Year bring about divine judgment and also forgiveness because of the merit of the fathers. Israel must repent and return to the Lord, who is merciful and will forgive them their sins. The penitential season of the New Year and Day of Atonement is the right time for confession and penitence, and God is sure to accept penitence. By exercising his power of mercy, the already-merciful God grows still stronger in mercy.

Third, God will save Israel personally at a time and circumstance of his own choosing. Israel may know what the future redemption will be like, because of the redemption from Egypt. The paradox of the red cow, that what imparts uncleanness—namely, touching the ashes of the red cow—produces cleanness is part of God's ineffable wisdom, which man cannot fathom. Only God can know the precise moment of Israel's redemption. That is something man cannot find out on his own. But God will certainly fulfil the predictions of the prophets about Israel's coming redemption. The Exodus from Egypt is the paradigm of the coming redemption. Israel has lost Eden—but can come home, and, with God's help, will. God's unique power is shown through Israel's unique suffering. In God's own time, he will redeem Israel.

To develop this point, the authorship proceeds to further facts, worked out in its propositional discourses. The lunar calendar, particular to Israel, marks Israel as favored by God, for the new moon signals the coming of Israel's redemption, and the particular new moon that will mark the actual event is that of Nisan. When God chooses to redeem Israel, Israel's enemies will have no power to stop him, because God will force Israel's enemies to serve Israel, because of Israel's purity and loyalty to God. Israel's enemies are punished, and what they propose to do to Israel, God does to them. Both directly and through the prophets, God is the source of true comfort, which he will bring to Israel. Israel thinks that God has forsaken them. But it is Israel who forsook God, God's love has never failed, and will never fail. Even though he has been angry, his mercy still is near and God has the power and will to save Israel. God has designated the godly for himself and has already promised to redeem them. He will assuredly do so. God personally is the one who will comfort Israel. While Israel says there is no comfort, in fact, God will comfort Israel. Zion/Israel is like a barren woman, but Zion will bring forth children, and Israel will be comforted. Both God and Israel will bring light to Zion, which will give light to the world. The rebuilding of Zion will be a source of joy for the entire world, not for Israel alone. God will rejoice in Israel, Israel in God, like bride and groom.

There is a profoundly cogent statement made through the composition of this document, and this is the message of Pesiqta deRab Kahana:

God loves Israel, that love is unconditional, and Israel's response to God must be obedience to the religious duties that God has assigned, which will produce merit. God is reasonable and when Israel has been punished, it is in accord with God's rules. God forgives penitent Israel and is abundant in mercy. God will save Israel personally at a time and circumstance of his own choosing. Israel may know what the future redemption will be like, because of the redemption from Egypt. Pesiqta deRab Kahana therefore has been so assembled as to exhibit a viewpoint, a purpose of its particular authorship, one quite distinctive, in its own context (if not in a single one of its propositions!) to its framers or collectors and arrangers.

Pesiqta deRab Kahana Pisqa Six

VI:I.

1. A. *If I were hungry, I would not tell you, for the world and all that is in it are mine. [Shall I eat the flesh of your bulls or drink the blood of he-goats? Offer to God the sacrifice of thanksgiving and pay your vows to the Most High. If you call upon me in time of trouble, I will come to your rescue and you shall honor me]* (Ps. 50:12–15):
   B. Said R. Simon, "There are thirteen traits of a merciful character that are stated in writing concerning the Holy One, blessed be he.
   C. "That is in line with this verse of Scripture:*The Lord passed by before him and proclaimed, the Lord, the Lord, God, merciful and gracious, long-suffering and abundant in goodness and truth; keeping mercy unto the thousandth generation, forgiving iniquity, transgression, and sin, who will by no means clear the guilty* (Exod. 34:6–7).
   D. "Now is there a merciful person who would hand over his food to a cruel person [who would have to slaughter a beast so as to feed him]?
   E. "One has to conclude: *If I were hungry, I would not tell you.*"
2. A. Said R. Judah bar Simon, "Said the Holy One, blessed be he, 'There are ten beasts that are clean that I have handed over to you [as valid for eating], three that are subject to your dominion, and seven that are not subject to your dominion.
   B. "'Which are the ones that are subject to your dominion? *The ox, sheep, and he-goat* (Deut. 14:4).
   C. "'Which are the ones not subject to your dominion? *The hart, gazelle, roebuck, wild goat, ibex, antelope, and mountain sheep* (Deut. 14:5).
   D. "'Now [in connection with the sacrificial cult] have I imposed on you the trouble of going hunting in hills and mountains to bring before me an offering of one of those that are not in your dominion?'
   E. "'Have I not said to you only to bring what is in your dominion and what is nourished at your stall?'
   F. "Thus:*If I were hungry, I would not tell you.*"

3.   A.   Said R. Isaac, "It is written, *[The Lord spoke to Moses and said, Give this command to the Israelites:] See that you present my offerings, the food for the food offering of soothing odor, to me at the appointed time. [Tell them: This is the food offering which you shall present to the Lord: the regular daily whole offering of two yearling rams without blemish. One you shall sacrifice in the morning and the second between dusk and dark]* (Num. 28:1–4).

      B.   "Now is there any consideration of eating and drinking before me?

      C.   "'Should you wish to take the position that indeed there is a consideration of eating and drinking before me, derive evidence to the contrary from my angels, derive evidence to the contrary from my ministers: . . .*who makes the winds your messengers, and flames of fire your servants'* (Ps. 104:4).

      D.   "Whence then do they draw sustenance? From the splendor of the Presence of God.

      E.   "'For it is written, *In the light of the presence of the King they live'*" (Prov. 16:15).

      F.   R. Haggai in the name of R. Isaac: *"You have made heaven, the heaven of heavens . . . the host . . . and you keep them alive"* (Neh. 9:6), meaning, you provide them with livelihood [Leon Nemoy, cited by Braude and Kapstein, p. 125, n. 4].

4.   A.   Said R. Simeon b. Laqish, "It is written, *This was the regular whole offering made at Mount Sinai, a soothing odor, a food offering to the Lord* (Num. 28:6).

      B.   "[God says] 'Now is there any consideration of eating and drinking before me?'

      C.   "'Should you wish to take the position that indeed there is a consideration of eating and drinking before me, derive evidence to the contrary from Moses, concerning whom it is written, *And he was there with the Lord for forty days and forty nights. Bread he did not eat, and water he did not drink'* (Exod. 34:28).

      D.   "Did he see me eating or drinking?

      E.   "Now that fact yields an argument a fortiori: now if Moses, who went forth as my agent, did not eat bread or drink water for forty days, is there going to be any consideration of eating and drinking before me?

      F.   "Thus: *If I were hungry, I would not tell you."*

5.   A.   Said R. Hiyya bar Ba, "Things that I have created do not need [to derive sustenance] from things that I have created, am I going to require sustenance from things that I have created?

      B.   "'Have you ever in your life heard someone say, 'Give plenty of wine to this vine, for it produces a great deal of wine'?

      C.   "'Have you ever in your life heard someone say, 'Give plenty of oil to this olive tree, for it produces a great deal of oil'?

      D.   "Things that I have created do not need [to derive sustenance] from things that I have created, am I going to require sustenance from things that I have created?

E. "Thus: *If I were hungry, I would not tell you.*"

6. A. Said R. Yannai, "Under ordinary circumstances if someone passes though the flood of a river, is it possible for him to drink a mere two or three *logs* of water? [Surely not. He will have to drink much more to be satisfied.]

B. "[God speaks:] 'But as for me, I have written that a mere single *log* of your wine shall I drink, and from that I shall derive full pleasure and satisfaction.'"

C. R. Hiyya taught on Tannaite authority, "*The wine for the proper drink offering shall be a quarter of a hin for each ram; you are to pour out this strong drink in the holy place as an offering to the Lord* (Num. 28:7).

D. "This statement bears the sense of drinking to full pleasure, satisfaction, and even inebriation."

7. A. Yosé bar Menassia in the name of R. Simeon b. Laqish, "When the libation was poured out, the stoppers [of the altar's drains] had to be stopped up [Braude and Kapstein, p. 126: so that the wine overflowing the altar would make it appear that God could not swallow the wine fast enough]."

B. Said R. Yosé bar Bun, "The rule contained in the statement made by R. Simeon b. Laqish is essential to the proper conduct of the rite [and if the drains are not stopped up, the libation offering is invalid and must be repeated]."

8. A. [God speaks:] "I assigned to you the provision of a single beast, and you could not carry out the order. [How then are you going to find the resources actually to feed me? It is beyond your capacity to do so.]

B. "And what is that? *It is the Behemoth on a thousand hills*" (Ps. 50:10).

C. R. Yohanan, R. Simeon b. Laqish, and rabbis:

D. R. Yohanan said, "It is a single beast, which crouches on a thousand hills, and the thousand hills produce fodder, which it eats. What verse of Scripture so indicates? *Now behold Behemoth which I made . . . Surely the mountains bring him forth food*" (Job 40:15).

E. R. Simeon b. Laqish said, "It is a single beast, which crouches on a thousand hills, and the thousand hills produce all sorts of food for the meals of the righteous in the coming age.

F. "What verse of Scripture so indicates? *Flocks shall range over Sharon and the Vale of Achor be a pasture for cattle; they shall belong to my people who seek me*" (Isa. 65:10).

G. Rabbis said, "It is a single beast, which crouches on a thousand hills, and the thousand hills produce cattle, which it eats.

H. "And what text of Scripture makes that point? *And all beasts of the field play there*" (Job 40:20).

I. But can cattle eat other cattle?

J. Said R. Tanhuma, *"Great are the works of our God* (Ps. 111:2), how curious are the works of the Holy One, blessed be he."

K. And whence does it drink?

L. It was taught on Tannaite authority: R. Joshua b. Levi said, "Whatever the Jordan river collects in six months, it swallows up in a single gulp.

M. "What verse of Scripture indicates it? *If the river is in spate, he is not scared, he sprawls at his ease as the Jordan flows to his mouth"* (Job 40:23).

N. Rabbis say, "Whatever the Jordan river collects in twelve months, it swallows up in a single gulp.

O. "What verse of Scripture indicates it? *he sprawls at his ease as the Jordan flows to his mouth* (Job 40:23).

P. "And that suffices merely to wet his whistle."

Q. R. Huna in the name of R. Yosé: "It is not even enough to wet his whistle."

R. Then whence does it drink?

S. R. Simeon b. Yohai taught on Tannaite authority, *"And a river flowed out of Eden* (Gen. 2:10), and its name is Yubal, and from there it drinks, as it is said, *That spreads out its roots by Yubal"* (Jer. 17:8).

T. It was taught on Tannaite authority in the name of R. Meir, *"But ask now the Behemoth* (Job 12:7)—this is *the Behemoth of the thousand hills* (Ps. 50:10), *and the fowl of the heaven will tell you* (Job 12:7), that is the ziz-bird (Ps. 50:10), *or speak to the earth that it tell you* (Job 12:8)—this refers to the Garden of Eden. Or *let the fish of the sea tell you* (Job 12:8)—this refers to Leviathan.

U. *"Who does not know among all these that the hand of the Lord has done this"* (Job 12:9).

9. A. "I gave you a single king, and you could not provide for him. [How then are you going to find the resources actually to feed me? It is beyond your capacity to do so.] And who was that? It was Solomon, son of David."

B. *The bread required by Solomon in a single day was thirty cors of fine flour and sixty cors of meal* (1 Kings 4:22).

C. Said R. Samuel bar R. Isaac, "These were kinds of snacks. But as to his regular meal, no person could provide it: *Ten fat oxen* (1 Kings 4:23), fattened with fodder, *and twenty oxen out of the pasture and a hundred sheep* (1 Kings 5:3), also out of the pasture; *and harts, gazelles, roebucks, and fatted fowl"* (1 Kings 4:23).

D. What are these fatted fowl?

E. R. Berekhiah in the name of R. Judah said, "They were fowl raised in a vivarium."

F. And rabbis say, "It is a very large bird, of high quality, much praised, which would go up and be served on the table of Solomon every day."

G. Said R. Judah bar Zebida, "Solomon had a thousand wives, and every one of them made a meal of the same dimensions as this meal. Each thought that he might dine with her."

H. "Thus: *If I were hungry, I would not tell you.*"

10. A. "One mere captive I handed over to you, and you could barely sustain him too. [How then are you going to find the resources actually to feed me? It is beyond your capacity to do so.]"

B. And who was that? It was Nehemiah, the governor:

C. *Now that which was prepared for one day was one ox and six choice sheep, also fowls were prepared for me, and once in ten days store of all sorts of wine; yet for all this I demanded not the usual fare provided for the governor, because the service was heavy upon this people* (Neh. 5:18).

D. What is *the usual fare provided for the governor?*

E. Huna bar Yekko said, "[Braude and Kapstein, p. 114:] It means gourmet food carefully cooked in vessels standing upon tripods."

F. "Thus: *If I were hungry, I would not tell you.*"

11. A. It has been taught on Tannaite authority: **The incense is brought only after the meal** (M. Ber. 6:6).

B. Now is it not the case that the sole enjoyment that the guests derive from the incense is the scent?

C. Thus said the Holy One, blessed be he, "My children, among all the offerings that you offer before me, I derive pleasure from you only because of the scent: *the food for the food offering of soothing odor, to me at the appointed time.*

The passage commences with what is clearly the contrastive verse, Ps. 50:12, which stands in stark contrast to the base verse, Num. 28:1ff., because what the latter requires, the former denigrates. No. 1 is open-ended, in that it does not draw us back to the base verse at all. It simply underlines one meaning to be imputed to the contrastive verse. No. 2 pursues the theme of the base verse—the selection of beasts for the altar—and reverts to the intersecting one. Nos. 3, 4, and 5 then draw us back to the base verse, but in a rather odd way. They treat it as simply another verse awaiting consideration, not as the climax of the exercise of explication of the many senses of the contrastive verse. The purpose of the composition before us is not to explore the meanings of the contrastive verse, bringing one of them to illuminate, also, the base verse. The purpose of the composition before us is to make a single point, to argue a single proposition, through a single-minded repertoire of relevant materials, each of which makes the same point as all the others. We may say that if a principal interest of the components of Leviticus Rabbah is exegetical, another principal interest, syllogistic, the sole interest of our authorship in the type of form before us is to invoke a contrastive verse to make the point that the base verse must be shown to establish. Before explaining the implications of that simple fact, let me complete the review of the whole.

I see no. 5 as the conclusion of the main event, that is to say, the contrastive verse has laid down its judgment on the sense of the base verse and established the syllogism. No. 6 then underlines that single point by saying that the natural world presents cases in which considerable volumes of food or drink are necessary to meet this-worldly requirements. How then can we hope to meet the supernatural requirements of God? That point, made at nos. 6, 8, 9, and 10, is essentially secondary to what has gone before. So we have a composition of two elements, nos. 1–5, the systematic exposition of the base verse in terms of the single proposition of the interesting verse, then nos. 6–10, the secondary point that reenforces the main one. No. 11 resolves the enormous tension created by the contrast between the base verse and the contrastive verse. I do not need the food, but I get pleasure from the smell.

Let me now revert to the main formal point at hand. If, therefore, we were to draw a contrast between the contrastive verse-base verse construction as we know it in Leviticus Rabbah and the counterpart before us, we should have to see them as essentially different modes of organizing and expressing an idea. The difference may be stated very simply. Leviticus Rabbah's compositors draw on materials that systematically expound the intersecting verse in a variety of ways, and only then draw back to the base verse to impute to it a fresh and unusual sense, invited by one of the several possible interpretations laid out by the intersecting verse. The framers of Pesiqta deRab Kahana, by contrast, draw upon a contrastive verse in order to make a point—one point—which then is placed into relationship with the base verse and which imposes its meaning on the base verse. What this means is that our document aims at making a single point, and at doing so with a minimum of obfuscation through exploration of diverse possibilities. The function of the contrastive verse is not to lay forth a galaxy of hermeneutical possibilities, one of which will be selected. It is, rather, to present a single point, and it is that point that we shall then impose upon our base verse. What that fact means, overall, is that our document aims at a syllogism, expressed singly and forcefully, rather than at a diversity of explanation of a verse that, in the end, will yield a syllogism. The difference between Leviticus Rabbah's intersecting verse-base-verse construction and Pesiqta deRab Kahana's contrastive verse-base-verse construction is sharp and total. The form—one verse, then another verse—looks the same. But the deeper structure is utterly unrelated.

VI:II

1. A. *A righteous man eats his fill [but the wicked go hungry]* (Prov. 13:25):
   B. This refers to Eliezer, our father Abraham's servant, as it is said, *Please let me have a little water to drink from your pitcher* (Gen. 24:17)—one sip.
   C. . . . but the wicked go hungry:
   D. This refers to the wicked Esau, who said to our father, Jacob, *Let me swallow some of that red pottage, for I am famished* (Gen. 25:30).
2. A. *[And Esau said to Jacob, Let me swallow some of that red pottage, for I am famished* (Gen. 25:30):]
   B. Said R. Isaac bar Zeira, "That wicked man opened up his mouth like a camel. He said to him, 'I'll open up my mouth, and you just toss in the food.'
   C. "That is in line with what we have learned in the Mishnah: **People may not stuff a camel or force food on it, but may toss food into its mouth** [M. Shab. 24:3]."
3. A. Another interpretation of the verse, *A righteous man eats his fill:*
   B. This refers to Ruth the Moabite, in regard to whom it is written, *She ate, was satisfied, and left food over* (Ruth 2:14).
   C. Said R. Isaac, "You have two possibilities: either a blessing comes to rest through a righteous man, or a blessing comes to rest through the womb of a righteous woman.
   D. "On the basis of the verse of Scripture, *She ate, was satisfied, and left food over,* one must conclude that a blessing comes to rest through the womb of a righteous woman."
   E. . . . *but the wicked go hungry:*
   F. This refers to the nations of the world.
4. A. Said R. Meir, "Dosetai of Kokhba asked me, saying to me, "What is the meaning of the statement, '. . . but the wicked go hungry?'
   B. "I said to him, 'There was a gentile in our town, who made a banquet for all the elders of the town, and invited me along with them. He set before us everything that the Holy One, blessed be he, had created on the six days of creation, and his table lacked only soft-shelled nuts alone.
   C. "What did he do? He took the tray from before us, which was worth six talents of silver, and broke it.
   D. "I said to him, 'On what account did you do this? [Why are you so angry?]'
   E. "He said to me, 'My lord, you say that we own this world, and you own the world to come. If we don't do the eating now, when are we going to eat [of every good thing that has ever been created]?'
   F. "I recited in his regard, . . . but the wicked go hungry."
5. A. Another interpretation of the verse, *A righteous man eats his fill [but the wicked go hungry]* (Prov. 13:25):
   B. This refers to Hezekiah, King of Judah.

C.   They say concerning Hezekiah, King of Judah, that [a mere] two
     bunches of vegetables and a *litra* of meat did they set before him every
     day.

D.   And the Israelites ridiculed him, saying, "Is this a king? *And they
     rejoiced over Rezin and Remaliah's son* (Isa. 8:6). But Rezin, son of
     Remaliah, is really worthy of dominion."

E.   That is in line with this verse of Scripture: *Because this people has
     refused the waters of Shiloah that run slowly and rejoice with Rezin and
     Remaliah's son* (Isa. 8:6).

F.   What is the sense of *slowly?*

G.   Bar Qappara said, "We have made the circuit of the whole of Scripture
     and have not found a place that bears the name spelled by the letters
     translated *slowly.*

H.   "But this refers to Hezekiah, King of Judah, who would purify the
     Israelites through a purification bath containing the correct volume of
     water, forty *seahs*, the number signified by the letters that spell the
     word for slowly."

I.   Said the Holy One, blessed be he, "You praise eating? *Behold the Lord
     brings up the waters of the River, mighty and many, even the king of
     Assyria and all his glory, and he shall come up over all his channels and
     go over all his banks and devour you as would a glutton*" (Isa. 8:7).

6.   A.   . . . *but the wicked go hungry*: this refers to Mesha.

     B.   *Mesha, king of Moab, was* a noked (2 Kings 3:4). What is the sense of
          noked? It is a shepherd.

     C.   "*He handed over to the king of Israel a hundred thousand fatted lambs
          and a hundred thousand wool-bearing rams*" (2 Kings 3:4).

     D.   What is the meaning of wool-bearing rams?

     E.   R. Abba bar Kahana said, "Unshorn."

7.   A.   Another interpretation of the verse, *A righteous man eats his fill [but
          the wicked go hungry]* (Prov. 13:25):

     B.   This refers to the kings of Israel and the kings of the House of David.

     C.   . . . *but the wicked go hungry* are the kings of the East:

     D.   R. Yudan and R. Hunah:

     E.   R. Yudan said, "A hundred sheep would be served to each one every
          day."

     F.   R. Hunah said, "A thousand sheep were served to each one every
          day."

8.   A.   Another interpretation of the verse, *A righteous man eats his fill* (Prov.
          13:25):

     B.   this refers to the Holy One, blessed be he.

     C.   Thus said the Holy One, blessed be he, "My children, among all the
          offerings that you offer before me, I derive pleasure from you only
          because of the scent: *the food for the food offering of soothing odor, to me
          at the appointed time.*"

Our contrastive verse now makes the point that the righteous one gets what he needs, the wicked go hungry, with a series of contrasts at nos. 1, 2, 3, 5, 6, 7, leading to no. 8: the Holy One gets pleasure from the scent of the offerings. I do not see exactly how the contrastive verse has enriched the meaning imputed to the base verse. What the compositors have done, rather, is to use the contrastive verse to lead to their, now conventional, conclusion, so 8.C appears tacked on as a routine conclusion, but, as before, turns out to be the critical point of cogency for the whole. Then the main point is that God does not need the food of the offerings; at most he enjoys the scent. The same point is made as before at VI:I.11: what God gets out of the offering is not nourishment but merely the pleasure of the scent of the offerings. God does not eat; but he does smell. The exegesis of Prov. 13:25, however, proceeds along its own line, contrasting Eliezer and Esau, Ruth and the nations of the world, Hezekiah and Mesha, Israel's kings and the kings of the East, and then God—with no contrast at all.

VI:III

1. A. *You have commanded your precepts to be kept diligently* (Ps.119:4):
    B. Where did he give this commandment? In the book of Numbers. [Braude and Kapstein, p. 132: *"In Numbers you did again ordain . . .* Where did God again ordain? In the Book of Numbers."]
    C. What did he command?
    D. *To be kept diligently* (Ps. 119:4): *The Lord spoke to Moses and said, Give this command to the Israelites: See that you present my offerings, the food for the food offering of soothing odor, to me at the appointed time.*
    E. That is the same passage that has already occurred [at Exod.29:38–42] and now recurs, so why has it been stated a second time?
    F. R. Yudan, R. Nehemiah, and rabbis:
    G. R. Yudan said, "Since the Israelites thought, 'In the past there was the practice of making journeys, and there was the practice of offering daily whole offerings. Now that the journeying is over, the daily whole offerings also are over.'
    H. "Said the Holy One, blessed be he, to Moses, 'Go, say to Israel that they should continue the practice of offering daily whole offerings.'"
    I. R. Nehemiah said, "Since the Israelites were treating the daily whole offering lightly, said the Holy One, blessed be he, to Moses, 'Go, tell Israel not to treat the daily whole offerings lightly.'"
    J. Rabbis said, "[The reason for the repetition is that] one statement serves for instruction, the other for actual practice."
2. A. R. Aha in the name of R. Hanina: "It was so that the Israelites should not say, 'In the past we offered sacrifices and so were engaged [in

studying about] them, but now that we do not offer them any more, we also need not study about them any longer.'

B. "Said the Holy One, blessed be he, to them, 'Since you engage in studying about them, it is as if you have actually carried them out.'"

3. A. R. Huna made two statements.

B. R. Huna said, "All of the exiles will be gathered together only on account of the study of Mishnah-teachings.

C. "What verse of Scripture makes that point? *Even when they recount [Mishnah-teachings] among the gentiles, then I shall gather them together*" (Hos. 8:10).

D. R. Huna made a second statement.

E. R. Huna said, "*From the rising of the sun even to the setting of the sun my name is great among the nations, and in every place offerings are presented to my name, even pure offerings* (Malachi 1:11). Now is it the case that a pure offering is made in Babylonia?

F. "Said the Holy One, blessed be he, 'Since you engage in the study of the matter, it is as if you offered it up.'"

4. A. Samuel said, "*And if they are ashamed of all that they have done, show them the form of the house and the fashion of it, the goings out and the comings in that pertain to it, and all its forms, and write it in their sight, that they may keep the whole form of it* (Ezek. 43:11).

B. "Now is there such a thing as the form of the house at this time?

C. "But said the Holy One, blessed be he, if you are engaged in the study of the matter, it is as if you were building it."

5. A. Said R. Yosé, "On what account do they begin instruction of children with the Torah of the Priests [the book of Leviticus]?

B. "Rather let them begin instruction of them with the book of Genesis.

C. "But the Holy One, blessed be he, said, 'Just as the offerings [described in the book of Leviticus] are pure, so children are pure. Let the pure come and engage in the study of matters that are pure.'"

6. A. R. Abba bar Kahana and R. Hanin, both of them in the name of R. Azariah of Kefar Hitayya: "[The matter may be compared to the case of] a king who had two cooks. The first of the two made a meal for him, and he ate it and liked it. The second made a meal for him, and he ate it and liked it.

B. "Now we should not know which of the two he liked more, except that, since he ordered the second, telling him to make a meal like the one he had prepared, we know that it was the second meal that he liked more.

C. "So too Noah made an offering and it pleased God: *And the Lord smelled the sweet savor* (Gen. 8:21).

D. "And Israel made an offering to him, and it pleased the Holy One, blessed be he.

E. "But we do not know which of the two he preferred.

F.   "On the basis of his orders to Israel, saying to them, *See that you present my offerings, the food for the food offering of soothing odor, to me at the appointed time*, we know that he preferred the offering of Israel [to that of Noah, hence the offering of Israel is preferable to the offering of the nations of the world]."

7.   A.   R. Abin made two statements.

B.   R. Abin said, "The matter may be compared to the case of a king who was reclining at his banquet, and they brought him the first dish, which he ate and found pleasing. They brought him the second, which he ate and found pleasing. He began to wipe the dish.

C.   *"I will offer you burnt offerings which are to be wiped off* (Ps. 66:15), like offerings that are to be wiped off I shall offer you, like someone who wipes the plate clean."

D.   R. Abin made a second statement:

E.   "The matter may be compared to a king who was making a journey and came to the first stockade and ate and drank there. Then he came to the second stockade and ate and drank there and spent the night there.

F.   "So it is here. Why does the Scripture repeat concerning the burnt offering: *This is the Torah of the burnt offering* (Lev. 3:5), *It is the burnt offering* (Lev. 6:2)? It is to teach that the whole of the burnt offering is burned up on the fires [yielding no parts to the priests]."

The rhetorical pattern now shifts. We have interest in the contrast between our base verse and another one that goes over the same matter. That contrast, to be sure, is invited by Ps. 119:4. But that contrastive verse does not function in such a way as to lead us to our base verse, but rather, as is clear, to lead us to the complementary verse for our base verse. That is, therefore, a different pattern from the one we have identified. The exegesis moves from text to context. We have two statements of the same matter, in Numbers and in Exodus, as indicated at no. 1. Why is the passage repeated? No. 1 presents a systematic composition on that question, no. 2 on another. No. 3 serves as an appendix to no. 2, on the importance of studying the sacrifices. But no. 3 obviously ignores our setting, since it is interested in the Mishnah-study in general, not the study of the laws of the sacrifices in particular. No. 4 goes on with the same point. No. 5 then provides yet another appendix, this one on the study of the book of Leviticus, with its substantial corpus of laws on sacrifice. No. 6 opens a new inquiry, this time into the larger theme of the comparison of offerings. It has no place here, but is attached to no. 7. That item is particular to Leviticus 6:2, but it concerns the same question we have here, namely, the repetition of statements about sacrifices, this time Lev. 3:5; 6:2. So nos. 6 and 7 are tacked on because of the congruence of the question, not the pertinence of the proposition. In that case we look to no. 1 for guidance, and there we find at issue the convergence of two verses on the same matter, and that is what stands behind our composition.

VI:IV

1. A. . . . *the regular daily whole offering of two yearling rams without blemish*:
   B. [Explaining the selection of the lambs,] the House of Shammai and the House of Hillel [offered opinions as follows:]
   C. The House of Shammai say, "Lambs are chosen because the letters that spell the word for lamb can also be read to mean that 'they cover up the sins of Israel,' as you read in Scripture: *He will turn again and have compassion upon us, he will put our iniquities out of sight*" (Micah 7:19).
   D. And the House of Hillel say, "Lambs are selected because the letters of the word lamb can yield the sound for the word *clean*, for they clean up the sins of Israel.
   E. "That is in line with this verse of Scripture: *If your sins are like scarlet, they will be washed clean like wool*" (Isa. 1:18).
   F. Ben Azzai says, ". . . *the regular daily whole offering of two yearling rams without blemish* are specified because they wash away the sins of Israel and turn them into an infant a year old."
2. A. [. . . *the regular daily whole offering of] two [yearling rams without blemish. One you shall sacrifice in the morning and the second between dusk and dark]*:
   B. *Two a day* on account of [the sins of] the day.
   C. *Two a day* to serve as intercessor for that day: *They shall be mine, says the Lord of hosts, on the day that I do this, even my own treasure, and I will spare them, as a man spares his son who serves him* (Malachi 3:17).
   D. *Two a day* meaning that they should be slaughtered in correspondence to that day in particular.
   E. *Two a day* meaning that one should know in advance which has been designated to be slaughtered in the morning and which at dusk.
3. A. . . . *a daily whole offering*:
   B. Said R. Yudan in the name of R. Simon, "No one ever spent the night in Jerusalem while still bearing sin. How so? The daily whole offering of the morning would effect atonement for the sins that had been committed overnight, and the daily whole offering of dusk would effect atonement for the transgressions that had been committed by day.
   C. "In consequence, no one ever spent the night in Jerusalem while still bearing sin.

D. "And what verse of Scripture makes that point? *Righteousness will spend the night in it*" (Isa. 1:21).

4. A. R. Judah bar Simon in the name of R. Yohanan: "There were three statements that Moses heard from the mouth of the Almighty, on account of which he was astounded and recoiled.

B. "When he said to him, *And they shall make me a sanctuary [and I shall dwell among them]* (Exod. 25:8), said Moses before the Holy One, blessed be he, 'Lord of the age, lo, the heavens and the heavens above the heavens cannot hold you, and yet you yourself have said, *And they shall make me a sanctuary [and I shall dwell among them]*.'

C. "Said to him the Holy One, blessed be he, 'Moses, it is not the way you are thinking. But there will be twenty boards' breadth at the north, twenty at the south, eight at the west, and I shall descend and shrink my Presence among you below.'

D. "That is in line with this verse of Scripture: *And I shall meet you there* (Exod. 25:20).

E. "When he said to him, *My food which is presented to me for offerings made by fire [you shall observe to offer to me]* (Num. 28:2), said Moses before the Holy One, blessed be he, 'Lord of the age, if I collect all the wild beasts in the world, will they produce one offering [that would be adequate as a meal for you]?

F. "'If I collect all the wood in the world, will it prove sufficient for one offering,' as it is said, *Lebanon is not enough for altar fire, nor the beasts thereof sufficient for burnt offerings* (Isa. 40:16).

G. "Said to him the Holy One, blessed be he, 'Moses, it is not the way you are thinking. But: *You shall say to them, This is the offering made by fire [two lambs of the first year without blemish, two day by day]* (Num. 28:3), and not two at a time but one in the morning and one at dusk, as it is said, *One lamb you will prepare in the morning, and the other you will prepare at dusk* (Num. 28:4).'

H. "And when he said to him, *When you give the contribution to the Lord to make expiation for your lives* (Exod. 30:15), said Moses before the Holy One, blessed be he, 'Lord of the age, who can give redemption-money for his soul?'

I. "'*One brother cannot redeem another* (Ps. 49:8), *for too costly is the redemption of men's souls* (Ps. 49:9).'

J. "Said the Holy One, blessed be he, to Moses, 'It is not the way you are thinking. But: *This they shall give*—something like this [namely, the half-shekel coin] they shall give."

The rhetorical pattern is clear: the base verse is analyzed, clause by clause. The point that is made is that the offerings achieve expiation and serve as intercessors. That is the same proposition that the contrastive verse wishes to establish. The exegesis of the components of the base verse accounts for the miscellany with which our *pisqa* draws to a close. But the point is cogent. The daily whole offering effects atonement for sins of the preceding day. No. 1 makes that point in one way, no. 2 in another. Deriving from elsewhere, no. 3, bearing in its wake no. 4, says the same thing yet a third time. So the miscellany is a composite but makes a single point in a strong way.

PART THREE

Parable and the Matrix of Scripture

THE RECAPITULATION OF SCRIPTURE
IN THE HERE AND NOW

11
Prologue

THE EVERYDAY AS RECAPITULATION
OF SCRIPTURE, SCRIPTURE AS
THE MATRIX FOR THE EVERYDAY

Sages in Midrash-compilations addressed transcendent issues of philosophy and paraphrase, theology and prophecy. But they also and especially wanted to know what God wanted of us in the here and now of everyday life. For if God is going to write me a letter, I want to hear about not only the sense of Scripture and its message, about not only holy Israel and its future, but also about how things are this morning. And that brings us to a reading of Scripture in the here and the now of my everyday life.

But that should not mean that the application of Scripture to the everyday will yield the ordinary and the familiar. Quite to the contrary, when the sages of Midrash-exegesis read Scripture as a parable for the ordinary and the familiar, they transform not Scripture into what is commonplace, but what is routine into the extraordinary framework of what is not. For one example, they teach how to find in the everyday a parable for the transcendent, and so the commonplace turns out to provide a metaphor for the wholly other. This is just the opposite of the way in which we are used to reading Scripture. Commonly, we read Scripture for its message to us. We do not read ourselves and our circumstances as a means for making sense of Scripture. But that is precisely what in Midrash-exegesis the sages accomplish.

Midrash-exegesis therefore mediates between the Holy Scriptures of ancient Israel and the living age. The way of doing so forms a paradigm. To understand what Midrash as parable means, let us review the earlier formations of Midrash-exegesis: paraphrase and prophecy. First, as we saw in part 1, Midrash says what Scripture says. Scripture therefore defines the permissible limits of Midrash, and, by implication, of all interpretation. Valid biblical interpretation says only what Scripture says: paraphrase and application. The hermeneutical implication is that in principle exegesis constitutes paraphrase enlivened by wit, erudition, free association.

Second, Midrash stands for disciplined association, something people discover about their own times in the encounter with a given verse, read wholly out of a defining and limiting context. In this way Midrash yields prophecy.

But, third, I find the ultimate meaning of Midrash in its message about who we are in relationship to God: in the search for proportion and balance between—in theological terms—our reason and God's revelation, our power to understand and God's power to instruct. Midrash mediates, and that is its meaning. Midrash, properly understood, lays down a position on that recurrent, anguished question: Precisely what does it mean for us mortals to be "in our image, after our likeness"? That is the ultimate parable: to see ourselves in God's likeness.

Midrash as parable shows us how the Judaic sages mediated between God's word and their own world, finding bridges from the one to the other, invoking the one as a metaphor—commonly, in parabolic form— for the other: equally and reciprocally. They learned from Scripture about what it meant for humanity to be "in our image, after our likeness," and they learned in the difficult world in which they lived how life in God's image of humanity, as Scripture set forth that image, was to be not only endured but lived in full holiness: the godly life on earth (in the language of Judaism), God incarnate (in the language of Christianity), life as the imitation of God (in language shared by both).

Scripture read in the prism of Midrash forms a commentary on everyday life. But, equally important, everyday life brings with it fresh understanding of Scripture. Midrash reads the one in the light of the other, imparting one meaning to both, drawing each toward the plane of the other. Midrash reads the everyday as the metaphor against which the eternal is to be read, and the eternal as the metaphor against which the everyday is to be reenacted. It is exemplified in the powerful reading of Genesis by Genesis Rabbah, of Leviticus by Leviticus Rabbah, in both cases bringing to Scripture the anguish and the terror of difficult times— and learning from Scripture God's plan and program for all times. That is what it means to read the everyday in the metaphor of the eternal. The deep structure of human existence, framed by Scripture and formed out of God's will as spelled out in the Torah, forms the foundation of our everyday life. Here and now, in the life of the hour, we can and do know

God. So everyday life forms a commentary on revealed Scripture—on the Torah—and Scripture, the Torah, provides a commentary on everyday life. Life flows in both directions. The sages who created the Midrash-compilations found in Scripture the story of the day at hand, which, they anticipated, would indeed form the counterpart and conclusion to the story of beginnings. They exercised a freedom of interpretation, by insisting that God speaks through the Torah to Israel everywhere and continually. And this meant that out of their own experience of the world, they also could interpret Scripture. To give a concrete example of that fact, I return to the Ten Commandments. But these are now read in a quite amazing way, as a parable of God's love for Israel. In Song of Songs Rabbah we see the profoundly parabolic reading of Scripture that draws upon everyday experience— indeed, experience of a most intimate kind, the love between man and woman—as a medium for reading Scripture and making sense of it for the here and now. So, as I said, the bridge formed by Midrash-exegesis brought traffic in both directions, from today to Sinai, from Sinai to the present moment.

12

Song of Songs Rabbah

GOD'S LOVE FOR US

Song of Songs (in the Christian Bible, "Song of Solomon") finds a place in the Torah, so Judaism has always maintained, because the collection of love songs in fact speaks about the relationship between God and Israel. What this means in fact is that Midrash-exegesis turns to everyday experience—the love of husband and wife—for a metaphor for God's love for Israel and Israel's love for God. Then, when Solomon's song says, ""O that you would kiss me with the kisses of your mouth! For your love is better than wine" (Song 1:2), our sages of blessed memory think of how God kissed Israel.

The key here is the word "your mouth," which bears the sense of communication, instruction, and a variety of broader meanings that all together add up to revelation. Then sages invoke Sinai, with special reference to the revelation of the Ten Commandments. The upshot is that God's love for Israel, his kisses, are the Ten Commandments. In this amazing reading of Song 1:2 we see in rich and detailed way precisely what it means to read Scripture as parable, to invoke our own experience of the everyday as a metaphor for the meaning of the Torah.

Song of Songs Rabbah to Song 1:2

II:I

1 A. "O that you would kiss me with the kisses of your mouth! For your love is better than wine]:"
   B. In what connection was this statement made?
   C. R. Hinena b. R. Pappa said, "It was stated at the sea: '[I compare you, my love] to a mare of Pharaoh's chariots'" (Song 1:9).
   D. R. Yuda b. R. Simon said, "It was stated at Sinai: 'The song of songs' (Song 1:1)—the song that was sung by the singers: 'The singers go before, the minstrels follow after'" (Ps. 68:26).

2. A. It was taught on Tannaite authority in the name of R. Nathan, "The Holy One, blessed be he, in the glory of his greatness said it: 'The song of songs that is Solomon's' (Song 1:1),

   B. "[meaning] that belongs to the King to whom peace belongs."

3. A. Rabban Gamaliel says, "The ministering angels said it: 'the song of songs' (Song 1:1)—

   B. "the song that the princes on high said."

4. A. R. Yohanan said, "It was said at Sinai: 'O that you would kiss me with the kisses of your mouth!'" (Song 1:2).

5. A. R. Meir says, "It was said in connection with the tent of meeting."

   B. And he brings evidence from the following verse: "Awake, O north wind, and come, O south wind! Blow upon my garden, let its fragrance by wafted abroad. Let my beloved come to his garden, and eat its choicest fruits" (Song 4:16).

   C. "Awake, O north wind:" this refers to the burnt offerings, which are slaughtered at the north side of the altar.

   D. "and come, O south wind:" this refers to the peace offerings, which were slaughtered at the south side of the altar.

   E. "Blow upon my garden:" this refers to the tent of meeting.

   F. "let its fragrance by wafted abroad:" this refers to the incense offering.

   G. "Let my beloved come to his garden:" this refers to the Presence of God.

   H. "and eat its choicest fruits:" this refers to the offerings.

6. A. Rabbis say, "It was said in connection with the house of the ages [the Temple itself]."

   B. And they bring evidence from the same verse: "Awake, O north wind, and come, O south wind! Blow upon my garden, let its fragrance by wafted abroad. Let my beloved come to his garden, and eat its choicest fruits" (Song 4:16).

   C. "Awake, O north wind:" this refers to the burnt offerings, which are slaughtered at the north side of the altar.

   D. "and come, O south wind:" this refers to the peace offerings, which are slaughtered at the south side of the altar.

   E. "Blow upon my garden:" this refers to the house of the ages.

   F. "let its fragrance by wafted abroad:" this refers to the incense offering.

   G. "Let my beloved come to his garden:" this refers to the Presence of God.

   H. "and eat its choicest fruits:" this refers to the offerings.

   I. The rabbis furthermore maintain that all the other verses also refer to the house of the ages.

   J. Said R. Aha, "The verse that refers to the Temple is the following: 'King Solomon made himself a palanquin, from the wood of Lebanon. He made its posts of silver, its back of gold, its seat of purple; it was lovingly wrought within by the daughters of Jerusalem'" (Song 3:9–10).

K. "Rabbis treat these as the intersecting verses for the verse, 'And it came to pass on the day that Moses had made an end of setting up the tabernacle'" (Num. 7:1).

7. A. In the opinion of R. Hinena [1.C], who said that the verse was stated on the occasion of the sea [the sense of the verse, "O that you would kiss me with the kisses of your mouth"] is, "may he bring to rest upon us the Holy Spirit, so that we may say before him many songs."

B. In the opinion of Rabban Gamaliel, who said that the verse was stated by the ministering angels [the sense of the verse, "O that you would kiss me with the kisses of your mouth"] is, "may he give us the kisses that he gave to his sons."

C. In the opinion of R. Meir, who said that the verse was stated in connection with the tent of meeting [the sense of the verse, "O that you would kiss me with the kisses of your mouth"] is, "May he send fire down to us and so accept his offerings."

D. In the opinion of R. Yohanan, who said that the verse was stated in connection with Sinai [the sense of the verse, "O that you would kiss me with the kisses of your mouth"] is, "May he cause kisses to issue for us from his mouth.

E. "That is why it is written, 'O that you would kiss me with the kisses of your mouth.'"

No. 7 once again shows us that our compilers are first-class editors, since they have assembled quite disparate materials and drawn them together into a cogent statement. But the subject is not our base verse, and hence the compilers cannot have had in mind the need of a commentary of a verse-by-verse principle of conglomeration and organization. The passage as a whole refers in much more general terms to the Song of Songs, and hardly to Song 1:2 in particular. That is shown by the simple fact that various opinions invoke other verses than the one to which the whole is ultimately assigned. No. 1 serves Song 1:1, and so does no. 2. Indeed, no. 2 could have been placed in the prior assembly without any damage to its use and meaning. The same is to be said for no. 3. In fact, only Yohanan requires the verse to stand where it now does. No. 5 and no. 6 of course invoke Song 4:16 and do a fine job of reading that verse in light of the tent of meeting in the wilderness or the Temple in Jerusalem. Song 3:9–10 serves as an appropriate locus as well. Then the conclusion draws a variety of senses for Song 1:2 alone, and that conclusion points to the compilers of the whole for its authorship. This is once more a highly sophisticated work of compilation, involving rich editorial intervention indeed.

II:II

1. A. Another interpretation of the verse, "O that you would kiss me with the kisses of your mouth:"

   B. Said R. Yohanan, "An angel would carry forth the Word [the Ten Commandments] from before the Holy One, blessed be he, word by word, going about to every Israelite and saying to him, 'Do you accept upon yourself the authority of this Word? There are so and so many rules that pertain to it, so and so many penalties that pertain to it, so and so many decrees that pertain to it, and so are the religious duties, the lenient aspects, the stringent aspects, that apply to it. There also is a reward that accrues in connection with it.'

   C. "And the Israelite would say, 'Yes.'

   D. "And the other would go and say to him again, 'Do you accept the divinity of the Holy One, blessed be he.'

   E. "And the Israelite would say, 'Yes, yes.'

   F. "Then he would kiss him on his mouth.

   G. "That is in line with this verse: 'To you it has been shown, that you might know' (Deut. 4:25)—that is, by an angel."

   H. Rabbis say, "It was the Word itself that made the rounds of the Israelites one by one, saying to each one, 'Do you accept me upon yourself? There are so and so many rules that pertain to me, so and so many penalties that pertain to me, so and so many decrees that pertain to me, and so are the religious duties, the lenient aspects, the stringent aspects, that apply to me. There also is a reward that accrues in connection with me.'

   I. "And the Israelite would say, 'Yes.' [Delete the words that can be translated 'for Adqulain son of Hadimah'].

   J. "So he taught him the Torah.

   K. "That is in line with this verse: 'Lest you forget the things your eyes saw' (Deut. 4:9)—how the Word spoke with you."

2. A. Another explanation of the phrase, "Lest you forget the things your eyes saw" (Deut. 4:9):

   B. The Israelites heard two acts of speech from the mouth of the Holy One, blessed be he.

3. A. [Reverting to no. 1:] R. Joshua b. Levi said, "The scriptural foundation for the position of rabbis is that after all the commandments, it then is written, 'You speak with us, and we will hear'" (Exod. 20:16).

   B. How does R. Joshua b. Levi explain this verse?

   C. He rejects the view that temporal order does not pertain to the Torah.

   D. Or perhaps the statement, "You speak with us and we will hear" applies only after every two or three of the Ten Commandments.

4. A. R. Azariah and R. Judah b. R. Simon in the name of R. Joshua b. Levi took his position. They said, "It is written, 'Moses commanded us the Torah' (Deut. 33:4).

B. "In the entire Torah there are six hundred thirteen commandments.
    The numerical value of the letters in the word 'Torah' is only six
    hundred eleven. These are the ones that Moses spoke to us.

C. "But 'I [am the Lord your God]' and 'You will not have [other gods
    besides me]' (Exod. 20:1–2) we have heard not from the mouth of
    Moses but from the mouth of the Holy One, blessed be he.

D. "That is in line with this verse: 'O that you would kiss me with the
    kisses of your mouth.'"

5. A. How did the Word issue forth from the mouth of the Holy One,
        blessed be he?

    B. R. Simeon b. Yohai and rabbis:

    C. R. Simeon b. Yohai says, "It teaches that the Word came forth from
        the right hand of the Holy One, blessed be he, to the left hand of the
        Israelites. It then made the round and circumambulated the camp of
        Israel, a journey of eighteen miles by eighteen miles, and then went
        and returned from the right hand of Israel to the left hand of the Holy
        One, blessed be he.

    D. "The Holy One, blessed be he, received it in his right hand and
        incised it on the tablets, and the sound went from one end of the world
        to the other: 'The voice of the Lord hews out flames of fire'" (Ps.
        29:7).

    E. Rabbis say, "But is there a consideration of 'left' above? And is it not
        written, 'Your right hand, O Lord, is glorious in power, your right
        hand, O Lord' (Exod. 15:6)?

    F. "But the Word came forth from the mouth of the Holy One, blessed
        be he, from his right hand to the right hand of Israel. It then made the
        round and circumambulated the camp of Israel, a journey of eighteen
        miles by eighteen miles, and then went and returned from the right
        hand of Israel to the right hand of the Holy One, blessed be he.

    G. "The Holy One, blessed be he, received it in his right hand and
        incised it on the tablets, and the sound went from one end of the world
        to the other: 'The voice of the Lord hews out flames of fire'" (Ps.
        29:7).

6. A. Said R. Berekhiah, "R. Helbo repeated to me the tradition that the
        Word itself was inscribed on its own, and when it was inscribed, and
        the sound went from one end of the world to the other: 'The voice of
        the Lord hews out flames of fire' (Ps. 29:7).

    B. "I said to R. Helbo, 'And lo, it is written, "written with the finger of
        God" (Exod. 31:18)?'

    C. "He said to me, 'Strangler! Are you thinking of strangling me?'

    D. "I said to him, 'And what is the sense of this verse: "tables of stone,
        written with the finger of God" (Exod. 31:18)?'

    E. "He said to me, 'It is like a disciple who is written, with the master's
        hand guiding his hand.'"

7. A. R. Joshua b. Levi and rabbis:
    B. R. Joshua b. Levi says, "Two Words [two of the Ten Commandments] did the Israelites hear from the mouth of the Holy One, blessed be he: 'I' and 'you will not have other gods, besides me' (Exod. 20:1–2), as it is said, 'O that you would kiss me with kisses of your mouth,' some, but not all of the kisses [commandments]."
    C. Rabbis say, "All of the Words did the Israelites hear from the mouth of the Holy One, blessed be he."
    D. R. Joshua of Sikhnin in the name of R. Levi: "The scriptural basis for the position of sages is the following verse of Scripture: 'And they said to Moses, Speak with us, and we will hear'" (Exod. 20:16).
    E. How does R. Joshua b. Levi interpret the verse?
    F. He differs, for considerations of temporal order do not apply in the Torah.
    G. Or perhaps the statement, "You speak with us and we will hear" applies only after every two or three of the Ten Commandments.

8. A. R. Azariah and R. Judah b. R. Simon in the name of R. Joshua b. Levi took his position. They said, "It is written, 'Moses commanded us the Torah' (Deut. 33:4).
    B. "In the entire Torah there are six hundred thirteen commandments. The numerical value of the letters in the word 'Torah' is only six hundred eleven. These are the ones that Moses spoke to us.
    C. "But 'I [am the Lord your God]' and 'You will not have [other gods besides me]' (Exod. 20:1–2) we have heard not from the mouth of Moses but from the mouth of the Holy One, blessed be he.
    D. "That is in line with this verse: 'O that you would kiss me with the kisses of your mouth.'"

9. A. R. Yohanan interpreted the verse ["O that you would kiss me with the kisses of your mouth"] to speak of the Israelites when they went up to Mount Sinai:
    B. "The matter may be compared to the case of a king who wanted to marry a woman, daughter of good parents and noble family. He sent to her a messenger to speak with her. She said, 'I am not worthy to be his serving girl. But I want to hear it from his own mouth.'
    C. "When that messenger got back to the king, [Simon:] his face was full of smiles, but what he said was not grasped by the king.
    D. "The king, who was astute, said, 'This one is full of smiles. It would appear that she has agreed. But what he says is not to be understood by me. It appears that she has said, 'I want to hear it from his own mouth.'
    E. "So the Israelites are the daughter of good parents. The messenger is Moses. The king is the Holy One, blessed be he.
    F. "At that time: 'And Moses reported the words of the people to the Lord' (Exod. 19:8).

G. "Then why say, 'And Moses told the words of the people to the Lord' (Exod. 19:9)?

H. "Since it says, 'Lo, I come to you in a thick cloud, so that the people may hear when I speak to you, and may also believe you forever' (Exod. 19:9), therefore, 'And Moses told the words of the people to the Lord' (Exod. 19:9).

I. "He said to him, 'This is what they have asked for.'

J. "He said to him, 'They tell a child what he wants to hear.'"

10. A. R. Phineas in the name of R. Levi said, "There is a proverb that people say: 'One who has been bitten by a snake is afraid even of a rope.'

B. "So said Moses, 'Yesterday, when I said, "But behold, they will not believe me" (Exod. 4:1), I got what was coming to me on their account. [He was struck by leprosy (Simon, p. 25, n. 3).] Now what am I going to do for them?'"

11. A. It was taught on Tannaite authority by R. Simeon b. Yohai, "This is what they asked.

B. "They said, 'We want to see the glory of our King.'"

12. A. R. Phineas in the name of R. Levi: "It was perfectly obvious before the Holy One, blessed be he, that the Israelites were going to exchange his glory for another: 'They exchanged their glory for the likeness of an ox that eats grass' (Ps. 106:20).

B. "Therefore [Simon, p. 25: he left them no excuse for saying] so that they might not say, 'If he had shown us his glory and greatness, we should certainly have believed in him, but now that his glory and greatness has not been shown to us, we do not believe in him.'

C. "This confirms the following: 'And enter not into judgment with your servant'" (Ps. 143:2).

13. A. R. Yudan in the name of R. Judah b. R. Simon, R. Judah, and R. Nehemiah:

B. R. Judah says, "When the Israelites heard, 'I am the Lord your God' (Exod. 20:1), the study of the Torah was fixed in their hearts, and they would study and not forget.

C. "They came to Moses saying, 'Our lord, Moses, you serve as inter-mediary, the messenger between us' [and God]: 'You speak with us, and we will hear' (Exod. 20:16), '. . . now therefore why should we die? (Deut. 5:25). Who gains if we perish?'

D. "Then they would study and forget what they have learned.

E. "They said, 'Just as Moses is mortal and passes on, so his learning passes away.'

F. "Then they came again to Moses, saying to him, 'Our lord, Moses, would that he would reveal it to us a second time.' 'O that you would kiss me with the kisses of your mouth!' 'Would that the learning of Torah would be set in our hearts as it was before.'

G. "He said to them, 'That cannot be now, but it will be in the age to come.'

H. "For it is said, 'I will put my Torah in their inner part, and on their heart I shall write it'" (Jer. 31:33).

I. R. Nehemiah said, "When the Israelites heard the word, 'You will not have other gods besides me,' the impulse to do evil was uprooted from their hearts.

J. "They came to Moses and said to him, 'Our lord, Moses, you serve as intermediary, the messenger between us' [and God]: 'You speak with us, and we will hear' (Exod. 20:16), '. . . now therefore why should we die? (Deut. 5:22). Who gains if we perish?'

K. "Forthwith the impulse to do evil came back.

L. "Then they came again to Moses, saying to him, 'Our lord, Moses, would that he would reveal it to us a second time.' 'O that you would kiss me with the kisses of your mouth!'

G. "He said to them, 'That cannot be now, but it will be in the age to come.'

H. "For it is said, 'And I will take away the stony heart out of your flesh'" (Ezek. 36:26).

14. A. R. Azariah, and some say R. Eliezer and R. Yosé b. R. Hanina and rabbis:

B. R. Eliezer says, "The matter may be compared to the case of a king who had a wine cellar.

C. "The first guest came to him first, and he mixed a cup for him and gave it to him.

D. "A second came and he mixed a cup for him and gave it to him.

E. "When the son of the king came, he gave him the whole cellar.

F. "So the First Man was commanded in respect to seven commandments.

G. "That is in line with this verse: 'And the Lord God commanded the man, saying, You may freely eat of every tree of the garden, but of the tree of the knowledge of good and evil you shall not eat, for in the day that you eat of it you shall die'" (Gen. 2:16).

15. A. ["And the Lord God commanded the man, saying, 'You may freely eat of every tree of the garden [but of the tree of the knowledge of good and evil you shall not eat, for in the day that you eat of it you shall die]'" (Gen. 2:16).]

B. [Gen. R. XVI:VI.1B adds:] R. Levi said, "He made him responsible to keep six commandments.

C. "He commanded him against idolatry, in line with this verse: 'Because he willingly walked after idols' (Hos. 5:11).

D. "'The Lord' indicates a commandment against blasphemy, in line with this verse: 'And he who blasphemes the name of the Lord' (Lev. 24:16).

E. "'God' indicates a commandment concerning setting up courts [and a judiciary]: 'You shall not revile the judges' [in the verse at hand, 'God'] (Exod. 22:27).

F. "'. . . the man' refers to the prohibition of murder: 'Whoever sheds man's blood' (Gen. 9:6).

G. "'. . . saying' refers to the prohibition of fornication: 'Saying, "If a man put away his wife"'" (Jer. 3:1).

H. "'Of every tree you may eat' (Gen. 2:16) indicates that he commanded him concerning theft. [There are things one may take, and there are things one may not take.]"

16. A. [Continuing Eliezer's statement, 14.G:] "As to Noah, a further commandment was assigned to him, not eating a limb cut from a living animal: 'Only flesh with the life thereof which is the blood thereof' (Gen. 9:4).

B. "As to Abraham, a further commandment was assigned to him, circumcision.

C. "Isaac devoted the eighth day to that rite.

D. "As to Jacob, a further commandment was assigned to him, the prohibition of the sinew of the thigh vein: 'Therefore the children of Israel do not eat the sinew of the thigh vein' (Gen. 32:33).

E. "As to Judah, a further commandment was assigned to him, levirate marriage: 'And Judah said to Onan, Go into your brother's wife and perform the duty of a husband's brother for her' (Gen. 38:8).

F. "The Israelites, by contrast, made their own all of the religious duties, positive and negative alike."

17. A. R. Yosé b. R. Hanina and rabbis say, "The matter may be compared to the case of a king who was divvying up rations to his legions through his generals, officers, and commanders.

B. "But when the turn of his son came, he gave him his rations with his own hand."

18. A. R. Isaac says, "The matter may be compared to a king who was eating sweetmeats,

B. "and when the turn of his son came, he gave him his rations with his own hand."

19. A. Rabbis say, "The matter may be compared to the case of a king who was eating meat.

B. "And when the turn of his son came, he gave him his rations with his own hand."

C. And some say, "He took it out of his mouth and gave it to him: 'For the Lord gives wisdom, out of his mouth comes knowledge and discernment'" (Prov. 2:6).

20. A. R. Abbahu, and some say the following in the name of R. Judah, and R. Nehemiah:

B. R. Nehemiah said, "[The matter of 'O that you would kiss me with the kisses of your mouth!' may be compared to] two colleagues who were occupied with teachings of the law. This one states a general principle of law, and that one states a general principle of law.

C. "Said the Holy One, blessed be he, 'Their source is through my power.' [Simon, p. 28: 'Their source comes from me.']

D. R. Judah said, "Even as to the breath that comes forth from one's mouth, as you say, 'But Job does open his mouth with a breath' (Job 35:16), said the Holy One, blessed be he, 'Their source is through my power.' [Simon, p. 28: 'Their source comes from me.']

E. Rabbis say, "The souls of these are going to be taken with a kiss."

21. A. Said R. Azariah, "We find that the soul of Aaron was taken away only with a kiss: 'And Aaron the priest went up to Mount Hor at the mouth of the Lord and died there' (Num. 33:38).

B. "How do we know the same in the case of the soul of Moses? 'So Moses the servant of the Lord died there . . . according to the mouth of the Lord' (Deut. 34:5).

C. "How do we know the same in the case of the soul of Miriam? 'And Miriam died there' (Num. 30:1). And just as 'there' in the former passage means 'by the mouth of the Lord,' so here too the fact is the same.

D. "But it would have been inappropriate to say it explicitly.

E. "How do we know the same in the case of the soul of all the righteous? 'O that you would kiss me with the kisses of your mouth!'

F. "[The sense is] 'If you have occupied yourself with teachings of the Torah, so that your lips are [Simon, p. 28:] well armed with them, then, at the end, everyone will kiss you on your mouth.'"

The whole point of including II:II.1.B through 4 is at 4.D. Without that reversion to the base verse, we must be mystified by the inclusion of the entire composition at this particular point, since it has no bearing upon the base verse at all. Yohanan's and sages' disagreement concerns whether an angel carried the Ten Commandments, or whether the Word—the Ten Commandments—went on its own. If we had to choose a base verse for the present composition, absent our base-verse of course, it would obviously have to be Deut. 4:25/Deut. 4:9. The interpolation of no. 2 may be ignored, and no. 3 expands on no. 1. No. 4 then is continuous with no. 3 and serves very well. So the whole has been composed in connection with the requirements of Deut. 4:9, 25, and then the revisions for insertion here are minimal. But that has not prevented the framers from adding on the immense secondary exposition of just how the Ten Commandments came out of God's mouth, nos.

5ff. The reason is not farfetched, however, since the base verse and the theme of the passage at hand surely justify raising such a secondary question of amplification. That is, if we read God's kisses as a reference to the Ten Commandments, then we are going to ask how the "kisses" came out of God's mouth. That accounts for the continuation at no. 7, with no. 8 tacked on as before. Nos. 9, 10, 11, 12, and 13 then carry forward the theme of the revelation at Sinai, introduced as it is by the verse at hand. No. 13 happens to appeal to our base verse, but that is in the context of an ongoing exposition, and the composition, which is first-class, cannot be credited to the ultimate redactors of our document merely because our base verse makes its appearance. The story can have worked very well without Song 1:2, and it is at least plausible that the base verse was inserted later on; it certainly does not flow within F, where it first occurs. Nos. 14 and 15 are thrown in to illustrate the greater intimacy implied in the words "his mouth," so Simon, p. 27, n. 4. While no. 15 continues the exposition of Gen. 2:16, which is integral to no. 14, it is in fact a free-standing composition, which is why I present it separately. But that requires duplicating Gen. 2:16 for clarity. Then no. 14 continues at nos. 16, 17, 18 and 19. I treat as distinct entries what is assigned to the others listed at 14.A. The point of no. 20 has no bearing on the foregoing, but it does address our base verse, now with a quite different focus. The point emerges only at the expansion of the point of no. 20.E in no. 21.

II:III

1. A. Another explanation of the verse, "O that you would kiss me with the kisses of your mouth! [For your love is better than wine]":
    B. "Let him arm me, purify me, make me cleave to him."
    C. "Let him arm me": "They were armed with bows and could use both the right hand and the left" (1 Chron. 12:2).
2. A. Said R. Simeon b. R. Nahman, "The words of Torah are to be compared to weapons.
    B. "Just as weapons protect their owners in wartime, so words of Torah protect those who work sufficiently hard at learning them."
    C. R. Hana b. R. Aha brings proof from the following verse for the same proposition: "'Let the high praises of God be in their mouth and a double-edged sword in their hand' (Ps. 149:6):
    D. "Just as a sword consumes on both its edges, so the Torah gives life in this world and life in the world to come."
3. A. R. Judah, R. Nehemiah, and rabbis:
    B. R. Judah says, "The Torah, which was said with one mouth, was said with many mouths."

C. R. Nehemiah said, "Two Torahs were stated, one by mouth, one in writing."

D. Rabbis say, "It is because they make a decree on creatures above and they do it, on creatures below and they do it." [Simon, p. 29: "(The Torah is said to have many mouths) because its students impose their will on the beings of the upper world and on the beings of the lower world."]

E. R. Joshua of Sikhnin in the name of R. Levi said, "The scriptural verse that supports the position of rabbis is as follows: 'For they were princes of holiness and princes of God' (1 Chron. 24:5).

F. "'princes of holiness': these are the ministering angels, thus: 'Therefore I have profaned the princes of the sanctuary' (Isa. 43:28).

G. "'and princes of God': this refers to Israel, thus, 'I said, "You are godlike beings"' (Ps. 82:6).

H. "'they make a decree on creatures above and they do it, on creatures below and they do it': for they carry out their deeds in a state of cultic cleanness."

The basic point here concerns the meanings to be imputed to the letters that spell out "kiss," and, as we know from the foregoing, among the available meanings is "arm." That accounts for the sense important at no. 1, which then accounts for the addition of no. 2. No. 3 then works on the notion that the Torah has many mouths, provoked by the introduction of the Torah as a double-edged sword.

II:IV

1. A. Another explanation of the verse, "O that you would kiss me with the kisses of your mouth! [For your love is better than wine]":

B. "Let him purify me, make me cleave to him, let him kiss me."

C. "Let him purify me": like a man who joins together ["kisses"] the water in two cisterns to one another and makes them cleave together [and so forms of them a valid immersion pool].

D. That is in line with the usage in the following verse: "Like the joining of cisterns he joins it" (Isa. 33:4).

We now work on the sense of the consonants used for "kiss" that yield "run," "join." That accounts for no. 1, who runs water from cistern to cistern and so forms of the two a valid immersion pool for purifying unclean objects.

II:V

1. A. Another explanation of the verse, "O that you would kiss me with the kisses of your mouth":

B. "Let him kiss me, let him make me cleave to him."

      C.   That is in line with the usage in this verse: "The noise of the wings of the living creatures as they touched one another" (Ezek. 3:13).

2.   A.   Another explanation of the verse, "O that you would kiss me [with the kisses of your mouth]":

      B.   Let him make for me the sound of kissing with his mouth.

The interest now is in the sense of the consonants used for "cleave," shown in 1.C for B. No. 2 works on the simple sense of "kiss" that the same consonants produce.

II:VI

1.   A.   "For your love is better than wine:" **There we have learned in the Mishnah [following the version in the Mishnah, which differs slightly from the version before us:] Said R. Judah, "R. Ishmael asked R. Joshua as they were going along the road.**

      B.   **"He said to him, 'On what account did they prohibit cheese made by gentiles?'**

      C.   **"He said to him, 'Because they curdle it with rennet from carrion.'**

      D.   **"He said to him, 'And is not the rennet from a whole offering subject to a more stringent rule than rennet from carrion,' and yet they have said, 'A priest who is not squeamish sucks it out raw?' [That is not deemed an act of sacrilege, even though the priests have no right to any part of a whole offering; hence the rennet is deemed null. Why then take account of rennet in the present circumstance, which is, after all, of considerably less weight than the sin of sacrilege?]"**

      E.   For R. Simeon b. Laqish said, "They treated it as one who drinks from a dirty cup. While, on the one side, one may derive no benefit from such a cup that belongs to the cult, yet one also is not liable for having violated the rule against sacrilege in making use of that cup."

      F.   **[Lacking in Song:]** (But they did not concur with him and ruled, "It is not available for [the priests'] benefit, while it also is not subject to the laws of sacrilege.")

      G.   **[Lacking in Song:] [Judah resumes his narrative:]** "He went and said to him, 'Because they curdle it with rennet of calves sacrificed to idols.**

      H.   **[Lacking in Song:]** "He said to him, 'If so, then why have they not also extended the prohibition affecting it to the matter of deriving benefit from it?'**

      I.   **"He moved him on to another subject.**

      J.   **"He said to him, 'Ishmael, my brother, How do you read the verse: "For your [masculine] love is better than wine," or, "Your [feminine] love is better than wine" (Song 1:2)?'**

      K.   **"He said to him, '"For your [feminine] love is better than wine."'**

      L.   **"He said to him, 'The matter is not so. For its neighbor teaches** concerning it, **"Your [masculine] ointments have a goodly fragrance"' (Song 1:3)"** [M. Abodah Zarah 2:5A-K].

M.   But why did he not tell him the reason [H, instead of just changing the subject, I]?

N.   Said R. Jonathan, "It is because it was only recently that they had made the ruling, and R. Ishmael was junior."

2.   A.   R. Simeon b. Halafta and R. Haggai in the name of R. Samuel b. R. Nahman: "It is written, 'The lambs will be for your clothing' (Prov. 27:26).

B.   "What is actually written may be read 'hidden,' yielding the meaning, 'When your disciples are junior, you should hear from them words of Torah. When they grow up and become disciples of sages, you may reveal to them the secrets of the Torah.'"

3.   A.   R. Simeon b. Yohai taught on Tannaite authority: "'Now these are the ordinances which you shall set before them' (Exod. 21:1).

B.   "[Since the consonants in 'set' may yield 'treasure,' we interpret in this way:] just as a treasure is not shown to anyone who comes along, so is the case with teachings of the Torah."

4.   A.   R. Huna raised the question, and R. Hama b. Uqba presented the same as an objection [to the response of 1.M to 1.H:] "If his intention was only to put him off, he should have put him off with one of the five equivalent points of unclarity in the Torah, which are [Simon, p. 31:] 'uplifting, cursed, tomorrow, almond-shaped, and arise.'

B.   "['uplifting:'] do we read 'If you do well, will it not be lifted up? (Gen. 4:7), or 'It is incurring sin if you do not do well'" (Gen. 4:7)? [That is another example of a point of unclarity in Scripture. He did not have to choose the one he chose. The others are not specified here.]"

C.   Said R. Tanhuma, "I have another [a sixth]: 'The sons of Jacob came in from the field when they heard it' (Gen. 34:7), or, 'When they heard it, the men were grieved' (Gen. 34:7–8) [so where is the break between the two sentences?]."

5.   A.   Said R. Isaac, "It is written, 'And me did the Lord command' (Deut. 4:14):

B.   "'There are matters that he said to me, all by myself, and there are matters that he said to me to say to his children.'"

6.   A.   [Following Simon, p. 31, n. 2, the point of reference in what follows is our base verse, "O that you would kiss me with the kisses of your mouth! For your love is better than wine"]: Said R. Ila, "There are matters about which one's [Simon:] lips are sealed. [Simon, p. 31, n. 2: It was for this reason that he put him off with the verse, because 'let him kiss me' may also mean, 'let him seal my lips,' and thus he hinted by this quotation that not everything is to be explained.]

B.   "How so? One verse of Scripture says, 'Your word have I laid up in my heart, that I might not sin against you' (Ps. 119:11), while another verse says, 'With my lips have I told all the ordinances of your mouth' (Ps. 119:13). How hold the two together?

C. "So long as Ira the Jairite was the master of David, he observed the verse, 'Your word have I laid up in my heart, that I might not sin against you' (Ps. 119:11), but after he died, then he followed this verse: 'With my lips have I told all the ordinances of your mouth'" (Ps. 119:13).

Here is a classic case of parachuting a complete composition that in no way serves the interests of a sustained reading of a base document. The only reason that this entire *talmud* has been inserted here—by *talmud* I mean a sustained discussion with its own dialectic and dynamic—is that our base verse forms part of the whole. But nothing that is said about our base verse fits together with any of the prevailing points of interest, let alone important propositions. But it is perfectly routine for framers of documents of the present type to collect everything they can in which the base verses appear, even though what they gather has been made up for purposes quite different from the ones that define the document under aggregation. We now move on to a separate theme, comparing "love" to words of Torah, with the sense of "love" as "loved ones," hence, "words of Torah."

II:VII

1. A. "For your love is better than wine":
    B. Words of Torah complement one another, friends of one another, close to one another,
    C. in line with the usage [of the consonants that are translated "love"] in the following verse: "or his uncle or his uncle's son" (Lev. 25:49).
2. A. [Supply: water removes uncleanness, when the water is of the correct classification:] "But a fountain or cistern wherein is a gathering of water" (Lev. 11:36).
    B. Water imparts susceptibility to uncleanness: "If water be put on seed" (Lev. 11:38). [The point of the juxtaposition is that while water can remove uncleanness, water can also impart susceptibility to uncleanness. The relationship of the two verses shows how words of Torah "complement one another, friends of one another, close to one another."]
3. A. Simeon b. R. Abba in the name of R. Yohanan: "Words of scribes are as precious as words of the Torah.
    B. "What is the scriptural basis for that view? [Following Simon:] 'And the roof of your mouth like the best wine' [Simon, p. 32, n. 3: The roof of the mouth is taken as a symbol of the oral Torah and wine as a symbol of the written Torah.]"
    C. Colleagues in the name of R. Yohanan: "Words of scribes are more

precious than words of Torah: 'For your love is better than wine' (Song 1:2).

D. "If one says, 'there is no requirement as to phylacteries,' so as to violate the requirements of the explicit words of the Torah, he is exempt from liability.

E. "If he says, 'There is a requirement that the phylacteries contain five [not four] compartments,' intending thereby to add to the requirements of the teachings of the scribes, by contrast, he is liable to a penalty."

4. A. R. Abba b. R. Kahana in the name of R. Judah b. Pazzi derived the same lesson from the following:

B. **Said R. Tarfon, "I was coming along the road [in the evening] and reclined to recite the Shema as required by the House of Shammai. And [in doing so] I placed myself in danger of [being attacked by] bandits." [They said to him, "You are yourself responsible (for what might have befallen you), for you violated the words of the House of Hillel."]** [M. Berakhot 1:3G-H].

C. You see that had he not recited the Shema at all, he would have violated a positive commandment alone. Now that he has recited the Shema, he has become liable for his life.

D. That proves that words of scribes are more precious than words of Torah.

5. A. R. Hanina b. R. Aha in the name of R. Tanhum b. R. Aha said, "They are subject to more stringent penalties than the words of the Torah and of the prophets.

B. "It is written, 'Do not preach, they preach' (Mic. 2:6). [Simon, p. 32, n. 9: implying that prophecy can be interrupted, but not so the teaching of the sages.]

C. "[The relationship of teachings of scribes and prophets] yields the following simile: the matter may be compared to the case of a king who sent his agents to a town. Concerning one of them he wrote, 'If he shows you my seal and signature, believe him, and if not, do not believe him,' and concerning the other of them he wrote, 'Even if he does not show you my seal and signature, believe him.'

D. "So in connection with teachings of prophecy: 'If there arise in your midst a prophet . . . and he gives you a sign' (Deut. 13:2).

E. "But as to words of scribes: 'According to the Torah that they will teach you' (Deut. 17:11).

F. "What is written is not, 'according to the Torah that the Torah will teach you,' but 'according to the Torah that they will teach you.'

G. "What is written is not, 'according to the judgment that it will tell you,' but, '. . . that they shall tell you.'

H. "Further: 'You shall not turn aside from the sentence that they shall declare to you to either the right hand or to the left' (Deut. 17:11):

I.   "If they tell you that the right hand is right and the left hand is left, obey; and even if they tell you that the right hand is left and the left hand is right!"

The point of nos. 1 and 2 is clear; no. 2 illustrates no. 1. The word for "love" is now under examination. A play on the word for "love" yields "roof of your mouth," and the entirety of what follows is tacked on for that reason. The point now is to compare the oral Torah with the written, and that forthwith yields the comparison of teachings of scribes ("sages" in Simon's translation) and teachings of the written Torah. We start with the claim that the two are equal, no. 3, and move on for the rest to the allegation that teachings of scribes or of the oral Torah are more to be valued and are subject to more severe penalties.

II:VIII

1. A.   Another explanation of the verse, "For your love is better than wine":
    B.   Words of the Torah are compared to water, wine, oil, honey, and milk.
2. A.   To water: "Ho, everyone who thirsts come for water" (Isa. 55:1).
    B.   Just as water is from one end of the world to the other, "To him who spread forth the earth above the waters" (Ps. 136:6), so the Torah is from one end of the world to the other, "the measure thereof is longer than the earth" (Job 11:9).
    C.   Just as water is life for the world, "A fountain of gardens, a well of living waters" (Song 4:15), so the Torah is life for the world, "For they are life to those who find them and health for all their flesh" (Prov. 4:22); "Come, buy and eat" (Isa. 55:1).
    D.   Just as water is from heaven, "At the sound of his giving a multitude of waters in the heavens" (Jer. 10:13), so the Torah is from heaven, "I have talked with you from heaven" (Exod. 20:19).
    E.   Just as water [when it rains] is with loud thunder, "The voice of the Lord is upon the water" (Ps. 29:3), so the Torah is with loud thunder, "And it came to pass on the third day, when it was morning, that there were thunderings and lightnings" (Exod. 19:16).
    F.   Just as water restores the soul, "But God cleaves the hollow place which was in Levi and water came out, and when he had drunk, he revived" (Judges 15:19), so the Torah [restores the soul], "The Torah of the Lord is perfect, restoring the soul" (Ps. 19:8).
    G.   Just as water purifies a person from uncleanness, "And I will sprinkle clean water upon you, and you will be clean" (Ezek. 36:25), so the Torah cleans a person of uncleanness, "The words of the Lord are pure" (Ps. 12:7).
    H.   Just as water cleans the body, "He shall bathe himself in water" (Lev. 17:15), so the Torah cleans the body, "Your word is purifying to the uttermost" (Ps. 119:140).

I. Just as water covers over the nakedness of the sea, "As the waters cover the sea" (Isa. 11:9), so the Torah covers the nakedness of Israel, "Love covers all transgressions" (Prov. 10:12).

J. Just as water comes down in drops but turns into rivers, so the Torah—a person learns two laws today, two tomorrow, until he becomes an overflowing river.

K. Just as water, if one is not thirsty, has no sweetness in it, so the Torah, if one does not labor at it, has no sweetness in it.

L. Just as water leaves the height and flows to a low place, so the Torah leaves one who is arrogant on account of [his knowledge of] it and cleaves to one who is humble on account of [his knowledge of] it.

M. Just as water does not keep well in utensils of silver and gold but only in the most humble of utensils, so the Torah does not stay well except in the one who treats himself as a clay pot.

N. Just as with water, a great man is not ashamed to say to an unimportant person, "Give me a drink of water," so as to words of Torah, the great man is not ashamed to say to an unimportant person, "Teach me a chapter," or "a verse," or even "a single letter."

O. Just as with water, when one does not know how to swim in it, in the end he will be swallowed up, so words of Torah, if one does not know how to swim in them and to give instruction in accord with them, in the end he will be swallowed up.

P. Said R. Hanina of Caesarea, "Just as water is drawn not only for gardens and orchards, but also for baths and privies, shall I say that that is so also for words of the Torah?

Q. "Scripture says, 'For the ways of the Lord are right'" (Hos. 14:10).

R. Said R. Hama b. Uqba, "Just as water makes plants grow, so words of the Torah make everyone who works in them sufficiently grow.

S. Then [may one say] just as water becomes rancid and smelly in a vessel, so words of the Torah are the same way? Scripture says that the Torah is like wine. Just as with wine, so long as it ages in the bottle, it improves, so words of the Torah, so long as they age in the body of a person, they improve in stature.

T. Then [may one say] just as water is not to be discerned in the body, so is the case with words of the Torah? Scripture says that the Torah is like wine. Just as with wine, its presence is discerned when it is in the body, so words of the Torah are discerned when they are in the body.

U. [For] people hint and point with the finger, saying, "This is a disciple of a sage."

V. Then [may one say] just as water does not make one happy, so is the case with words of the Torah? Scripture says that the Torah is like wine. Just as wine "makes the heart of man glad" (Ps. 104:15), so words of the Torah make the heart happy, "The precepts of the Lord are right, rejoicing the heart" (Ps. 19:9).

W. Then [may one say] just as wine sometimes is bad for the head and the body, so is the case with words of the Torah? Scripture compares words of the Torah to oil. Just as oil is pleasing for the head and body, so words of the Torah are pleasing for the head and body: "Your word is a lamp to my feet" (Ps. 119:105).

X. May one then say, just as oil is bitter to begin with, and sweet only at the end, so is it the case also with words of Torah? Scripture states, "Honey and milk" (Song 4:11). Just as they are sweet, so words of the Torah are sweet: "Sweeter than honey" (Ps. 19:10).

Y. May one then say, just as honey has wax cells [that cannot be eaten], so words of the Torah are the same? Scripture says, ". . . milk" (Song 4:11). Just as milk is pure, so words of the Torah are pure: "Gold and glass cannot equal it" (Job 28:17).

Z. May one then say, just as milk is [Simon:] insipid, so words of the Torah are the same? Scripture states, "Honey and milk" (Song 4:11). Just as honey and milk, when they are stirred together, do not do any harm to the body, so words of the Torah: "It shall be health to your navel" (Prov. 3:8); "For they are life to those who find them" (Prov. 4:22).

The composition is sustained and perfect. The comparison of "your love," understood as "words of the Torah," to wine persuaded the compositors that the entire piece belongs. But of course it has not been written out to serve our base verse in particular, nor any other as a matter of fact. It is a free-standing and powerful composition, making its own point about its own subject, and not an amplification, in terms of another set of values, of a given verse and its contents.

II:IX

1. A. Another explanation of the verse, "For your love is better":
    B. This refers to the patriarchs.
    C. "than wine":
    D. this refers to the princes.
2. A. Another explanation of the verse, "For your love is better":
    B. This refers to the offerings.
    C. "than wine":
    D. this refers to the libations.
3. A. Said R. Hanina, "If when the Israelites came to that awful deed, Moses had known how precious were the offerings, he would have offered all the offerings that are catalogued in the Torah.
    B. "Instead he ran to the merit of the patriarchs: 'Remember Abraham, Isaac, and Israel, your servants'" (Exod. 32:13).
4. A. Another explanation of the verse, "For your love is better":
    B. This refers to Israel.

C.   "than wine":

D.   this refers to the gentiles.

E.   [For the numerical value of the letters that make up the word for wine] is seventy,

F.   teaching you that the Israelites are more precious before the Holy One, blessed be he, than all the nations."

The composition, with its modest interpolation at no. 3, is a powerful triplet, in which the more valuable is compared with the less valuable, first patriarchs as against princes, then offerings as against merit, finally Israel as against the nations. That the whole is inseparable and unitary is shown by the climax, no. 4, and that becomes obvious because of the interpolation at no. 3. So the whole, inclusive of no. 3, is aiming at the final point, 4.F.

Epilogue

In the Torah God reaches us in words and in our response we make our worlds out of them. We who study Scripture as God's word for us are drawn to seek not only understanding but also faith and truth. Midrash forms one path to faith and truth. My argument in this anthology has been that this-worldly human experiences are shaped by the Torah into moments of revelation, and that the Torah attains its fullest meaning when our this-worldly human experiences impose sense and meaning upon revelation: context for the content of the Torah. Through Midrash, therefore, we precipitate theological reflection. Specifically, in the Midrash-compilations of the dual Torah we learn to see ourselves as metaphors and as similes: "in our image, after our likeness." To construct faith through Scripture is to explore the meaning of humanity viewed as image and likeness of something else, of life lived like metaphor: like an ongoing existence of *as if*. Midrash is a way of seeing life *as if*, and in the pages of this book I have tried to show what that mode of scriptural encounter must mean.

In turning to Scripture as mediated by Midrash, after all, I want to know not only the this-worldly testimony but the object of the testimony: the reality of God in the life of Torah, not alone the meaning of the words that point to or convey the reality. But understanding rests on learning, and faith seeks intelligence. A religious world without words to tell us in proposition and syllogism what is at hand lives only for the moment of its epiphany. But to what shall we compare a religious world composed only of words to tell us what we are because we are in God's image, after God's likeness? Relying only on reports of an experience out there, an encounter we have not ourselves had, is like a kiss through a veil, a poem in translation, a report about pain, a narrative of someone else's death. Midrash forms the royal road between a religious world made up only of dead words and a religious world comprised by only immediate experience. Midrash mediates. Midrash forms bridges. Midrash creates comparisons and through its transformation of Scripture allows us to encounter the Other, the wholly Other, who is God.

That explains why Midrash-exegesis and Midrash-compilation lay stress on the Torah as the living word of God. Judaism is a religion because through enchantment ordinary human experiences are transformed into metaphors of the sacred, enchantment being called, in the language of Judaism, sanctification. Precisely what I mean by life as metaphor is conveyed by Midrash-compilations we have examined: both Scripture as prophecy and Scripture as parable show us the vitality of our powers of analogy and comparison. And this leads to what I believe is the highest stake of all. It is how Midrash as a mode of receiving the Torah or studying Scripture imparts to us the knowledge of God.

Just as in the account of the creation of Man and Woman we are made "in our image, after our likeness," so, I argue, we stand for something more, as a metaphor, as a simile: like God. And this we do in most concrete reality, for each human experience represents a simile of the sacred and serves as a metaphor for the transformation of the given into a gift of God. Enchantment changes us from what we are to something more. Midrash then stands for the magic of the Torah, the magic and the mystery too. For Judaism as a religion treats life as an *as-if*, turns experience from an *is* to an *imagine what if*. And that transforms the ordinary into the holy. In the here and now of the workaday world, the same act of skilled imagination, the daring leap of the disciplined heart, shows us for what we are: metaphors of what it means to be "our image" and "our likeness." Of such things as us is God's image made of. How much has God loved us that through the Torah God has told us so.

The reason people today gain from access to Midrash, the ancient Judaic sages' religious reading of Scripture, is simple. In their time, place, and idiom, they worked out solutions to problems that, in our circumstances, continue to engage us. These problems are philosophical, theological, and moral, and so I lay out examples of Midrash-exegeses of Scripture that deal with problems of all three kinds. For we and they share the conviction that Scripture is God's word not then alone but also now, spoken not in time long gone but in and to our own age: to me, here and now. What does it mean to receive Scripture—the Torah—as God's word to my particular circumstance? To gain the answer, some pray, others reflect, but all Christians and Jews must begin by bringing themselves to Scripture, and Scripture to their own time and place. And, for both the sages and ourselves, that means the act of study. For study of those words of God, the Bible to Christians, the whole Torah to Jews, is the one palpable, this-worldly, and concrete testimony we have, and I think, all we have and all we shall ever have, to tell us

what God means by "in our image, after our likeness." For the Bible—
the Torah—these are after all God's words.

Learning therefore is the one act that joins Christian and Judaic
believers in our day and draws them close to one another in a common
act in service of one and the same God: *use of the mind to gain access to
God through God's word.*

Bibliography

TRANSLATIONS AND STUDIES OF MIDRASH-
COMPILATIONS BY JACOB NEUSNER

I. TRANSLATIONS OF MIDRASH-COMPILATIONS

Judaism and Scripture: The Evidence of Leviticus Rabbah. Chicago: University of Chicago Press, 1986 [fresh translation of Margulies' text].

Genesis Rabbah. The Judaic Commentary on Genesis. A New American Translation. Atlanta: Scholars Press for Brown Judaic Studies, 1985. I. *Genesis Rabbah: The Judaic Commentary on Genesis. A New American Translation. Parashiyyot One through Thirty-Three; Genesis 1:1—8:14.*

Genesis Rabbah: The Judaic Commentary on Genesis. A New American Translation. Atlanta: Scholars Press for Brown Judaic Studies, 1985. II. *Genesis Rabbah: The Judaic Commentary on Genesis. A New American Translation. Parashiyyot Thirty-Four through Sixty-Seven; Genesis 8:15—28:9.*

Genesis Rabbah: The Judaic Commentary on Genesis. A New American Translation. Atlanta: Scholars Press for Brown Judaic Studies, 1985. III. *Genesis Rabbah. The Judaic Commentary on Genesis. A New American Translation. Parashiyyot Sixty-Eight through One Hundred; Genesis 28:10—50:26.*

Sifra: The Judaic Commentary on Leviticus. A New Translation. The Leper: Leviticus 13:1—14:57. Chico: Scholars Press for Brown Judaic Studies, 1985 [with a section by Roger Brooks]. Based on *A History of the Mishnaic Law of Purities. VI. Negaim. Sifra.*

Sifré to Numbers: An American Translation. I. 1–58. Atlanta: Scholars Press for Brown Judaic Studies, 1986.

Sifré to Numbers: An American Translation. II. 59–115. Atlanta: Scholars Press for Brown Judaic Studies. 1986. [III. 116–161: William Scott Green.]

The Fathers according to Rabbi Nathan: An Analytical Translation and Explanation. Atlanta: Scholars Press for Brown Judaic Studies, 1986.

Pesiqta deRab Kahana: An Analytical Translation and Explanation. I. 1–14. Atlanta: Scholars Press for Brown Judaic Studies, 1987.

Pesiqta deRab Kahana. An Analytical Translation and Explanation. II. 15–28. *With an Introduction to Pesiqta deRab Kahana.* Atlanta: Scholars Press for Brown Judaic Studies, 1987.

For Pesiqta Rabbati, see below, *From Tradition to Imitation: The Plan and Program of Pesiqta deRab Kahana and Pesiqta Rabbati.*

Sifré to Deuteronomy: An Analytical Translation. Atlanta: Scholars Press for Brown Judaic Studies, 1987. I. *Pisqaot One through One Hundred Forty-Three. Debarim, Waethanan, Eqeb, Re'eh.*

Sifré to Deuteronomy: An Analytical Translation. Atlanta: Scholars Press for Brown Judaic Studies, 1987. II. *Pisqaot One Hundred Forty-Four through Three Hundred Fifty-Seven. Shofetim, Ki Tese, Ki Tabo, Nesabim, Ha'azinu, Zot Habberakhah.*

Sifré to Deuteronomy: An Introduction to the Rhetorical, Logical, and Topical Program. Atlanta: Scholars Press for Brown Judaic Studies, 1987.

Sifra: An Analytical Translation. Atlanta: Scholars Press for Brown Judaic Studies, 1988. I. *Introduction, Vayyiqra Dibura Denedabah, and Vayiqqra Dibura Dehobah.*

Sifra: An Analytical Translation. Atlanta: Scholars Press for Brown Judaic Studies, 1988. II. *Sav, Shemini, Tazria, Negaim, Mesora, and Zabim.*

Sifra: An Analytical Translation. Atlanta: Scholars Press for Brown Judaic Studies, 1988. III. *Aharé Mot, Qedoshim, Emor, Behar, and Behuqotai.*

Mekhilta Attributed to R. Ishmael: An Analytical Translation. Atlanta: Scholars Press for Brown Judaic Studies, 1988. I. *Pisha, Beshallah, Shirata, and Vayassa.*

Mekhilta Attributed to R. Ishmael: An Analytical Translation. Atlanta: Scholars Press for Brown Judaic Studies, 1988. II. *Amalek, Bahodesh, Neziqin, Kaspa, and Shabbata.*

Lamentations Rabbah: An Analytical Translation. Atlanta: Scholars Press for Brown Judaic Studies, 1989.

Esther Rabbah I: An Analytical Translation. Atlanta: Scholars Press for Brown Judaic Studies, 1989.

Ruth Rabbah: An Analytical Translation. Atlanta: Scholars Press for Brown Judaic Studies, 1989.

Song of Songs Rabbah: An Analytical Translation. Volume One, *Song of Songs Rabbah to Song Chapters One through Three.* Atlanta: Scholars Press for Brown Judaic Studies, 1990.

Song of Songs Rabbah: An Analytical Translation. Volume Two. *Song of Songs Rabbah to Song Chapters Four through Eight.* Atlanta: Scholars Press for Brown Judaic Studies, 1990.

II. STUDIES OF MIDRASH-COMPILATIONS IN LITERARY AND HISTORICAL CONTEXT

The Integrity of Leviticus Rabbah: The Problem of the Autonomy of a Rabbinic Document. Chico: Scholars Press for Brown Judaic Studies, 1985.

Comparative Midrash: The Plan and Program of Genesis Rabbah and Leviticus Rabbah. Atlanta: Scholars Press for Brown Judaic Studies, 1986.

From Tradition to Imitation: The Plan and Program of Pesiqta deRab Kahana and

Pesiqta Rabbati. Atlanta: Scholars Press for Brown Judaic Studies, 1987. [With a fresh translation of Pesiqta Rabbati *Pisqaot* 1-5, 15.]

Canon and Connection: Intertextuality in Judaism. Lanham: University Press of America, 1986. Studies in Judaism Series.

Midrash as Literature: The Primacy of Documentary Discourse. Lanham: University Press of America, 1987. Studies in Judaism Series.

Invitation to Midrash: The Working of Rabbinic Bible Interpretation. A Teaching Book. San Francisco: Harper & Row, 1988.

What Is Midrash? Philadelphia: Fortress Press, 1987.

Making the Classics in Judaism: The Three Stages of Literary Formation. Atlanta: Scholars Press for Brown Judaic Studies, 1990.

The Midrash Compilations of the Sixth and Seventh Centuries. An Introduction to the Rhetorical, Logical, and Topical Program. I. *Lamentations Rabbah.* Atlanta: Scholars Press for Brown Judaic Studies, 1990.

The Midrash Compilations of the Sixth and Seventh Centuries: An Introduction to the Rhetorical, Logical, and Topical Program. II. *Esther Rabbah I.* Atlanta: Scholars Press for Brown Judaic Studies, 1990.

The Midrash Compilations of the Sixth and Seventh Centuries: An Introduction to the Rhetorical, Logical, and Topical Program. III. *Ruth Rabbah.* Atlanta: Scholars Press for Brown Judaic Studies, 1990.

The Midrash Compilations of the Sixth and Seventh Centuries: An Introduction to the Rhetorical, Logical, and Topical Program. IV. *Song of Songs Rabbah.* Atlanta: Scholars Press for Brown Judaic Studies, 1990.

Judaism and Scripture: The Evidence of Leviticus Rabbah. Chicago: University of Chicago Press, 1986. [Systematic analysis of problems of composition and redaction.]

Judaism and Story: The Evidence of The Fathers According to Rabbi Nathan. Chicago: University of Chicago Press, 1990.

Uniting the Dual Torah: Sifra and the Problem of the Mishnah. Cambridge and New York: Cambridge University Press, 1989.

Sifra in Perspective: The Documentary Comparison of the Midrashim of Ancient Judaism. Atlanta: Scholars Press for Brown Judaic Studies, 1988.

Mekhilta Attributed to R. Ishmael: An Introduction to Judaism's First Scriptural Encyclopaedia. Atlanta: Scholars Press for Brown Judaic Studies, 1988.

Translating the Classics of Judaism: In Theory and in Practice. Atlanta: Scholars Press for Brown Judaic Studies, 1989.

The Foundations of Judaism: Method, Teleology, Doctrine. Philadelphia: Fortress Press, 1983-85. I-III. I. *Midrash in Context: Exegesis in Formative Judaism.* Second printing: Atlanta: Scholars Press for Brown Judaic Studies, 1988.

The Foundations of Judaism: Method, Teleology, Doctrine. Philadelphia: Fortress Press, 1983-85. I-III. III. *Torah: From Scroll to Symbol in Formative Judaism.* Second printing: Atlanta: Scholars Press for Brown Judaic Studies, 1988.

The Oral Torah: The Sacred Books of Judaism. An Introduction. San Francisco: Harper & Row, 1985. Paperback: 1987. B'nai B'rith Jewish Book Club Selection, 1986.

Editor: *Scriptures of the Oral Torah: Sanctification and Salvation in the Sacred Books of Judaism.* San Francisco: Harper & Row, 1987. Jewish Book Club Selection, 1988.

Editor: *Judaisms and their Messiahs in the Beginning of Christianity.* New York: Cambridge University Press, 1987. [Edited with William Scott Green and Ernest S. Frerichs.]

Judaism and Christianity in the Age of Constantine: Issues of the Initial Confrontation. Chicago: University of Chicago Press, 1987.

Writing with Scripture: The Authority and Uses of the Hebrew Bible in the Torah of Formative Judaism. Minneapolis: Fortress Press, 1989.

The Making of the Mind of Judaism. Atlanta: Scholars Press for Brown Judaic Studies, 1987.

Editor: *The Christian and Judaic Invention of History.* [Edited with William Scott Green]. Atlanta: Scholars Press for American Academy of Religion, 1989. Studies in Religion Series.

Why No Gospels in Talmudic Judaism? Atlanta: Scholars Press for Brown Judaic Studies, 1988.

Genesis and Judaism: The Perspective of Genesis Rabbah. An Analytical Anthology. Atlanta: Scholars Press for Brown Judaic Studies, 1986.

Christian Faith and the Bible of Judaism. Grand Rapids: Wm. B. Eerdmans, 1987.

Reading Scriptures: An Introduction to Rabbinic Midrash. With Special Reference to Genesis Rabbah. New York: Rossel, 1990.

From Testament to Torah: An Introduction to Judaism in its Formative Age. Englewood Cliffs: Prentice Hall, 1987.

General Index

Abba b. R. Kahana
  equality of priest and congregation, 109
  God revealing love, 157
  holy way of life, 130, 132
  prophesy, history and revelation, 82, 90
  sin, God hiding his face, 104
Abbahu
  God revealing love, 150
  prophesy, history and revelation, 83, 93
Abin, holy way of life, 133
Aha
  equality of priest and congregation, 106
  God revealing love, 143
  holy way of life, 131
  outwitting sin, 113
Ahai b. R. Josiah, commandments and
  God's law, 64
Aibu
  equality of priest and congregation, 110
  sin, God hiding his face, 104
Ammi, prophesy, history and revelation, 96
Appointed times and holy way of life, 120–
  136
Aqiba
  commandments and God's law, 65
  equality of priest and congregation, 106
  free-will offerings, 41
Azariah
  God revealing love, 145, 147, 149, 151
  prophesy, history and revelation, 86
Azariah of Kefar Hitayya, holy way of life,
  132

Bar Qappara, holy way of life, 130
Ben Azzai, holy way of life, 134
Berekhiah
  equality of priest and congregation,
  108–109
  God revealing love, 146
  holy way of life, 126
  prophesy, history and revelation, 92
Birai, prophesy, history and revelation, 90

Cleanness and uncleanness, 23–25
  free-will offerings, 39–48
Commandments and God's law, 51–67
  for now and age to come, 25–30
Constantine, Emperor, 71

Eleazar, equality of priest and
  congregation, 108, 111–12
Eleazar b. Hananiah b. Hezekiah b. Garon,
  commandments and God's law, 63
Eliezer
  commandments and God's law, 58
  equality of priest and congregation, 106,
  108–10
  God revealing love, 149
Equality of priest and congregation, 105–
  13

Free-will offerings, 39–48

Gamaliel, God revealing love, 143–44
Guilt offerings, 34–35

Haggai
  holy way of life, 124
  prophesy, history and revelation, 93
Hama b. Uqba, God revealing love, 155,
  159
Hana b. R. Aha, God revealing love, 152
Hanin, holy way of life, 132
Hanina
  equality of priest and congregation, 110
  God revealing love, 160
  holy way of life, 131
  sin, God hiding his face, 104
Hanina b. R. Aha, God revealing love, 157
Hanina b. Antigonus, commandments and
  God's law, 58
Hanina of Caesarea, God revealing love,
  159
Hanina of Sepphoris, prophesy, history and
  revelation, 96

169

Index of Biblical
and Talmudic References